From Shoo-ing Crows:

The Journey of

John Rogan, System Manager of South African Railways and Harbours

John Rogan

as told to

Margaret Rogan

Edited and published by Ruarri Mackenzie Rogan

For His Descendants. And Those To Come.

John Rogan
+Margaret Gillis Smith
── John Andrew Rogan
    +Anne Doris Wylie
        Allister John Rogan
        +Jennifer Gerder Wallace
            ── Katherine Anne Rogan
                +John Hulme Scholes
                    ── Anna Rogan Scholes
                    ── Rachel Katherine Scholes
            ── Nicola Jean Rogan
                +Philip Albert Myburgh
                    ── Alexandra Louise Myburgh
                    ── Tessa Irene Myburgh
                    ── Rachel Katherine Myburgh
                    ── Philip Albert Myburgh
            ── Donald Mackenzie Rogan
                +Judy Anne Libera
                    ── Nicholas John Rogan
                    ── Juliet Louise Rogan
                    ── Megan Ashley Rogan
            ── Robert Wallace Rogan
                +Anthea Buckham
                    ── James Mackenzie Rogan
        Ian Mackenzie Rogan
        +Kathleen Finegan
            ── Francis Anne Rogan
            ── Theresa Jean Rogan
            ── Ruarri Mackenzie Rogan
                +Jacqueline Rose Hunter
                    ── Ignatius Mackenzie Rogan
                    ── Montague Hunter Rogan
        Peter James Harold Rogan
        +Lorna Christina Rogan
            ── Alexander Peter Ian Rogan
                +Julia Helen Quarry
                    ── Fergus George Alexander Rogan
                    ── Romilly Josephine Wallace Rogan
            ── James Mackenzie Rogan
                +Jeanette Soleta Louise Merle Oliver
                    ── Rafael John Wilson Rogan
                    ── Eva Phoebe Jennifer Rogan
                    ── Leonardo Simon Peter Rogan
            ── Juliet Lorna Christina Rogan
                +Daniel Bovington
            ── Angela Doris Fiona Rogan
                +Stephen Fienberg
            ── Robert Leslie Rogan
── Mackenzie Stuart Rogan
── Harold Edwin Rogan
    +Emma Unsted
        John Mackenzie Rogan
        +Ann Ifft
            ── Michael Rogan
            ── Allyson Rogan
                ── Liam Klyve
                ── Emery Klyve
── Douglas Smith Rogan
    +Rosemary Middelton
        ── Anne Rogan
        ── Rodney Rogan
        ── Wendy Rogan

DEDICATED

to the

best and noblest of women:

MY WIFE

INDEX

Preface

*I*n the 68th year of my age, after completing an arduous, successful and happy railway career, I purpose, not without considerable hesitation, being deeply conscious of my limitations, to relate in autobiographical form the story, in realistic form, of my gradual upward advancement, extending over a period of some 50 years from the lowly agricultural work of shooing crows on a field of young turnips in the south of Scotland to the much coveted position of System Manager of Railways, on the South African Railways and Harbours in the mandated Territory of South West Africa.

My pathway was set with many seemingly unsurmountable difficulties, such as are encountered by most railwaymen, only a very few of whom ever reach the bottleneck extending from the senior clerical positions to the high administrative positions at the very top.

The work of compiling the autobiography is one of pleasure, and it is hoped that in the years which lie ahead our progeny will obtain much pleasure, and even profit in reading it.

Imagination has not been invited to embellish the simple narrative, and I have but inadequately expressed my love, amounting almost to adoration for our beautiful, sunny, happy, prosperous South Africa, where opportunity to advance awaits all who are willing to give of their best for the good of their fellowmen, irrespective of race, colour, or creed.

I realised my ambition to be a railwayman at the age of 17 years, and I have a storehouse full of happy memories in the service of the:

Caledonian Railway;

Cape Government Railways; and

The South African Railways and Harbours

but it is doubtful whether I would again choose a career demanding the best years of one's life in a struggle to reach a social and financial level where one can breathe freely and contentedly.

The narrative records that Mum and I come from esteemed, honest, industrious, God-fearing men and women who fearlessly faced up to life, which to them was an endless struggle under intolerable Tory (Capitalist) conditions, contributing nobly in their circumscribed spheres to the welfare of the communities in which they resided.

Equipped with only a meagre country-school education, lacking the valuable asset of a good personality, and not overly robust, I determined as a lad to succeed along the path of honest endeavour coupled with conscientious application to duty and God, honouring my honesty of purpose, from which I consistently refused to be deviated, elevated me to one of the topmost rungs in the Railway Service. To Him be all the Glory.

Ever since my conversion, my faith in God never wavered, His promises being ever before me:

> For promotion cometh neither from the East, nor from the West, nor from the South, but God is the judge: He putteth down one, and setteth up another.
>
> Psa. 75:6-7

> Wait on the Lord and keep His way
> and He shall exalt thee
>
> Psa. 37:34

> He will fulfil the desire of them
> that fear Him.
>
> Psa. 145:20

It is God which worketh in you both
to will and to do of his good pleasure.

Phil. 2:13

JOHN ROGAN

Johannesburg, 1948.

CHILDHOOD YEARS

In bracing air, with singing birds,
    and humming of the bees,
Children romp through wood and glen,
    'neath the leafy trees.
In morning air the lark ascends,
    with song both sweet and clear,
and workers sing in harvest field
    'midst scenes forever dear.
With swelling note the starlings sing,
    their joyous evening lay;
high on the trees the squirrels work
    throughout the summer day.
Blackbirds flit the garden round,
    their evening meals to claim,
And from the woods there echoes clear
    the cuckoo's sweet refrain.
In boyish glee, in twilight long,
    I scamper o'er the hill
And hear the curlew's homeward call
    in cry both high and shrill.
I listen to the music
    of the gurgling mountain stream
And see the startled wildduck rise
    from out the meadow green.
'Tween snowclad hills on lochs we skate,
    our cheeks with health aglow.
Rival teams at snowball play
    and chase far o'er the snow.
On snowclad trees, in moonlight pale,
    eerie hoots the owl,
And from deep lair, on side the hill,
    the wary foxes howl.
In springtime fresh, with blossoms sweet,
    in bracing, crisp, clean air,
The snowdrop on the lawn we greet
    in raiment pure and fair.

The trees and flowers spring into life
    and call us out to roam.
Life was sweet in childhood days
    in that sweet country home.
J.R.
March 1932

Editor's Note

This book is a Scottish immigrant's account of the first fifty years of the twentieth century in South Africa. It is the autobiography of John Rogan (1881-1955), my great-grandfather, typed out and bound numerous times by my great-grandmother, Margaret (1882-1981), who gifted it to each of their grandchildren. John was born a peasant. His journey from the Scottish peasantry to becoming a successful South African railwayman had profound consequences for our family. Most of his lineage now reside in South Africa and every subsequent generation of Rogan has lived a more comfortable life than he did, and that's thanks to him.

His account begins by detailing his formative years (1881-1900) as a young boy in rural Scotland, where the shadow of Robert the Bruce's fourteenth-century quest for Scottish independence still loomed. The significance of clan names stretches back to Robert the Bruce. And clan names, like Mackenzie, were interwoven into society through ties of blood and marriage. Margaret, who was a pure Scott, is the source of the Mackenzie namesake that runs as a first or a middle name through our family. Mackenzie, as a surname, signaled more prominence than Rogan and was more common among lairds than young lads. The Rogan name has humbler origins in Northern Ireland's peasants displaced and uprooted by the English during the Plantation of Ulster in the seventeenth century.

John's paternal grandfather, James Rogan, the son of Edward (born circa 1780), was born in Armagh, Ireland, around 1811. James left Armagh to work on the steel lines of Glasgow's railways. His journey ended in Roucan, Dumfriesshire, where he passed away in 1878, just three years before the birth of John. John's maternal great-grandfather, John (aka James) King, a weaver from Banbridge, County Down, Ireland, fought in the Battle of Waterloo (18 June, 1815).

John Rogan, raised in Roucan, experienced a world where change unfolded generation by generation. However, it was neither a bucolic nor a sheltered existence. As a boy, John was forced to do hard labour and played amidst the green knolls that concealed the mass graves of long-dead Scots, slaughtered and buried en masse for refusing to bow to papal authority.

Born at the end of the nineteenth century, John came of age in the twentieth—a century marked by an unprecedented pace of change. As a boy, John yearned for the world beyond Roucan—a world he hoped would carry him beyond agricultural toil. In his youth, he heard of the Boer War (16 December, 1880 – 23 March, 1881), which shook the foundations of the British Empire.

John left Scotland for South Africa in 1902. A mere baby during the First Boer War, he would come face to face with the fallout of the Second as a twenty-year-old, newly stationed deep in South Africa's interior, nearly 1000 kms from Cape Town, in Sterkstroom. John writes of his encounters with those displaced by the Second Boer War (11 October, 1899 – 31 May, 1902), "[t]he train loads of evacuees returning from the concentration camp at East London to their devastated farms and homes in the Orange Free State and Transvaal, were a sight, sorrowful, depressing and humiliating."

John's autobiography provides us with a window into a tumultuous and exciting period in history. He wrote this book in pre-apartheid South Africa at a time when the crumbling of the British Empire promised the birth of something new. In the years after the Great War (18 July, 1914 – 11 November, 1918), technology experienced a surge. Yet, progress was often accompanied by devastation, including the 1918 flu, which claimed the lives of millions. Every blessing seemed to come with a curse, and every curse was tinged with the promise of a blessing— Mandela was born on 18 July, 1918.

John saw the world darken in the lead-up to World War II (September 1, 1939 – September 2, 1945). Of his four children, only two survived the war years. John and Doug survived, Mackenzie and Harold did not. Mackenzie passed away childless. Harold left a son, John, behind, and his widowed wife was tasked with raising the boy alone. Doug, a fighter pilot who continued the fight even after losing his leg, returned to South Africa as a hero. Doug married and had children. John's firstborn, John Andrew (aka Ian), was spared the horrors of war and fathered three sons— Allister, Ian (aka Mack), and Peter.

After the war years, South Africa underwent significant changes. Apartheid's gloom spilled out into the world in 1948. However, John's writings convey that Apartheid was not predestined or welcomed by all. In his preface, he offers a glimpse of his optimism for an egalitarian South Africa. In his poem, "Natives," his early peasant roots are evident as he agonises over the fate of Black South Africans. He was one of many sympathisers.

This document is a part of John Rogan's legacy. In our ever-changing world, his tale grounds us. Facing substantial shifts in history, we can reflect on his story, breathe a sigh of relief, and silently intone, "'twas ever thus." His words impart lessons of gratitude, endurance, and resilience. We can learn much from him, and we all can take a page from his book.

Ruarri M. Rogan, October 2023.

Epilogue
The Natives

The natives of South Africa are held in economic slavery in a heartless, cold-blooded manner, and the churches look on in cold indifference, adopting an attitude like that of the American Churches towards the slaves prior to their emancipation.

The Natives

A cluster of huts, worn, tattered, lean,
Many within the neighbourhood seen.
Conditions grim, to satiate greed's eye,
Here, natives in squalor live and die.

Streets abound with wealth on each side,
Native children in humble hovels hide.
Indifferent, crowds rush to and fro,
Unmoved, they choose not to know.

Rich and thriving in this fertile land,
Whites luxuriate and wallow in golden sand.
The natives, a subjugated, oppressed race,
Of compassion for them, there is no trace.

A native child, in pain and laboured breath,
Seeks life, not the coldness of death.
In grief, the parents in despair do stare,
Unheeding, does the white man care?

Native children, transient they seem,
In unnamed graves, they silently dream.
A mother's sorrow, in simple attire clad,
It matters not, her heart is sad.

From dawn to dusk, natives toil,
Bound to a never-ending, weary coil.
Death approaches, their loss unseen,
Well-fed whites are oblivious to the scene.

We relish life; what of the native's dim
Existence in squalor, filth, and din?
We remain distant; it's not our role to cheer,
They persist and perish in dwellings drear.

Eternal God, Father to us all,
With earnest love, He does enthrall.
On Calvary's Cross, they walked on by,
Just another, condemned to die.

A Loving God, His grace the same,
A Universal Cross, a sacred flame.
All are precious, black and white,
In His love, we can all unite.

                    J.R.
                    Johannesburg,
                    16.9.1943

Prelude: My Early Environment

The peasants in the South of Scotland were a strong, vigorous, healthy people, kindly, loveable, and homely. The men, and not a few of the women, toiling in the fields, in all sorts of weather, from early morn till dusk. Everywhere they could be heard singing the "Aul' Scotch Sangs" and whistling as they worked on the lands, with folklore in the forefront of their conversations. The evenings were spent "aroun" the *ingle nook* [hearth] or working in the garden in the summer evenings.

The yoke laid upon these humble, happy people under an unsympathetic system of Tory landlordism was indeed grievous, the lairds and farmers treating their servants as the appointed hewers of wood and drawers of water and paying them a wage insufficient to enable the workers to live in a state of reasonable comfort.

My childhood was spent in a beautiful old-time hamlet called "The Roucan" in the parish of Torthorwald, 3½ miles from the town of Dumfries, in the South of Scotland, where many stirring local and national events took place during Scotland's "darkest hour".

The district was the scene of much savagery during the Reformation and the mounds of murdered saints, who refused to accept the "indulgences" offered by the church of Rome, preferring torture and the gibbet-bear eloquent testimony to the bravery unto death of the Protestant Scots in defence of their faith against Satan-inspired, Pope-directed murder and torture.

A mile to the North, Torthorwald Village nestled peacefully and comfortably on the side of the "Bank" hill with the village smithy with its sparks and forge fire, the meal mill with its large water wheel, the school, *manse and Kirk* [clergy house and church], not forgetting the ruins of the 11th Century castle with its crumbling turrets, large frameless windows, dried-up moat, and 11-foot-thick walls where the children loved to climb and explore. Here, the Kirkpatricks ruled with a fist of mail, surrounded by knights and served by serfs. Robert the Bruce, Liberator of Scotland from the English yoke and hero of the battle of Bannockburn, enjoyed hospitality within its walls, and brave knights, who could have been much better employed, sallied forth, followed by illiterate serfs to join in border forays.

Strange as it may seem in our day of National oneness, goodwill, and commercial intercourse, border forays were looked upon as "fair game", and cattle "rievers" considering themselves good, honest Scotchmen, resented English retaliation when they were worsted at their own game.

The large, barn-like old church, with a faraway-high, forbiddingly large pulpit, bore ample evidence of the large, thriving community of cottars and crofters, large and small farmers, weavers, shoemakers, cloggers, coopers, blacksmiths, and tailors who had populated the district. Now, alas, no more; the advent of agricultural machinery, the amalgamation of small farms having driven the workers from the land that they loved, to the towns and cities, where they were forced to live an unreal existence. We were told this had to be — that it resulted from economic laws, but I confess to a deepening conviction that it need not have been, and I am convinced Scotland is the poorer today because of this short-sighted, inhuman policy.

Moss-covered slab gravestones dating back to about the 11th Century may still be seen in the churchyard, reminder that "body snatching" was a regular night-time practice until the beginning of the 19th Century.

Each thatched cottage stood in a small, well-kept garden; moore and hills abounded in the district; glens through which the burns cascaded on their way to join the river Loch or meandering towards the Solway Firth and hedgerows fragrant with honeysuckle and wild roses formed a scene of perfect loveliness.

In summer, the woods were carpeted with bluebells, primrose covered the banks, the glens were resplendent in ferns and wildflowers, daisies grew in profusion in the fields, cultivated lands met the eye everywhere, and a sweet, tranquil, spiritual atmosphere pervaded and uplifted the hearts of the people.

In winter, the land generally lay under a covering of snow. The trees looked ghostly in the glistening snow; ice and frost held everything in their grasp and Nature was asleep.

With early Spring came the beautiful snow-white snowdrops, sometimes from under the snow. Everywhere, tree, hedge, and bush shot forth green buds, lambs sported on the knowes, and life sprang anew from the deadness of winter. Strong men with heavy loads sowed the rich grain, believing implicitly that God would reward their labours and that the harvest of golden grain would be rich—and it generally was.

Birds of many varieties and in great numbers abounded in the district: lark ascended in song to greet the rising sun; thrush sang gaily on the cool of the evening; swallow and swift zoomed overhead in the long summer twilight; and the plaintive call of the cuckoo floated through the air from nearby woods. The cry of the curlew, or Whaup, echoed over the moors, whilst the wren, robin, chaffinch, and a host of other birds twittered and chirped in every bush and tree.

In the woods the fox prowled and howled throughout the night; beautifully marked adders glided swiftly though the heather; in the moss, multicoloured butterflies flitted about everywhere and bees hummed from flower to flower. Rabbits played hide-and-seek around and through their burrows, a hare raced at great speed across fields, stopping ever and anon to look backwards, cattle browsed contentedly on the pasture lands, and horses strained their massive shoulders to their harness.

In the distance, the white sands and crested waves of the Solway Firth could be seen on a clear day, shimmering in the sun, with the Cumberland Hills enveloped in a soft blue haze in the background. It was on these sands that Edward I, King of England died in 1307, when on the march to wage aggressive war against Scotland. God, who is no respecter of persons, makes even the wrath of kings to give way before His holy will.

Men and women of all ages, from youth to hoary years, laboured blithely and strenuously in the fields from dawn to dusk, assisted not at all infrequently by children of tender years, of whom I was one from time to time.

The wages paid were extremely meagre to say the least: 15/- [15 shillings] per week earned by experienced men and half that amount by the women of proved worth. Holidays were never thought of for the peasants, and home comforts were considered unnecessary for peasants by the Lairds and farmers. At least, they did not pay their servants sufficient to enable them to enjoy anything outside the range of food and clothes.

Saving for sickness, old age, or unforeseen contingencies could not be done.

The children enjoyed themselves scampering barefoot in summer and autumn over daisy-carpeted fields, the boys guddling (catching trout with the hands, at which we were adept) in the burns, romping through the glens, playing in and around the bluebell-carpeted woods, listening to the feathered choirs and climbing the braes. We were fully in tune with Nature and listened with childish intent to the fairies singing in the bluebells.

Winter brought skating (called "sli-ing") with iron-shod clogs (we did not wear boots) on the icebound roads and dams, and snowballing, building snowmen, and the mor vigorous forms of games (we never spoke of sport) were indulged in with great zest and cheeks aglow.

Everything was provided by Nature to enable man to live in tune with Nature and God, in the power of the resurrected Lord, but Satan was active, using the Land-owners and farmers for his evil designs, and man, made in the image of God, was ground to the very dust with less consideration than was given to the horses and dogs who held first place in the affections of their owners.

It was to such people that Burns wrote:

> What though on hamely fare we dine,
> Wear hoddin grey, an' a that;
> Gie fools their silks, and knaves their wine;
> A Man's a Man for a' that:
> For a' that, and a' that,
> Their tinsel show, an' a' that;
> The honest man, tho' e'er sae poor,
> Is king o' men for a' that.
> A Man's A Man For A' That
> Robert Burns (1795)

The yoke of serfdom, perpetuated under the cloak of democracy, then in its infancy, lay heavy on the shoulders of the honest, stout-hearted peasants with soul-destroying, devastating effect more devilish, if more refined, than the brutality of African chiefs towards their servile tribesmen and -women. The latter could kill outright, while under the cloak of Christian

Civilization, agricultural labourers were slowly worn out with incessant toil and then cast off, perhaps to pine and die in the cold, soulless parish poorhouse.

In the absence of more than an elementary education, and an ever-present state of financial poverty, sons followed the plough in the footsteps of their fathers, and beautiful, sweet, rosy-cheeked (they did not need rouge) Scotch lassies were doomed to become domestic servants, dairymaids and general "slaveys" in the employ of farmers and others, whose daughters were generally sent to "schools for young ladies" to finish their education and prepare them for society life.

To quote Burns again:

A prince can mak a belted knight,
A marquis, duke, an' a' that;
But an honest man's aboon his might,
Guid faith he mauna fa' that!

A Man's A Man For A' That

Thus in an atmosphere of light-hearted singing, whistling, dancing, attending the annual parish fair, "gaan tae the Kirk" on Sundays, I grew up in the midst of some of the most beautiful scenery, probably in the world, considering myself fortunate indeed to be living in the Roucan, but with an ever-increasing resentment towards the overlords whose inhumanity and avariciousness permeated and deadened the family life of the workers.

It was indeed fortunate that I grew up in an atmosphere devoid of competition and thus unconscious of the severe handicaps, and that toiling in the fields during school holidays, from tender years, did not break my childish buoyancy of spirit, but I was resentful, suffering the injustices and hardships that I shared with all the others in open revolt.

Everything in this district related to ploughing, sowing, reaping, and preparing for the long, cold winter when a mantle of snow covered the Earth, and frost bound practically everything.

When the frost has gemmed "the bistie stibble field"
And a healthy nip is in the winter morn,
When the horses are strappin' free to the clankin'
swingle tree,
Then a plooman's wark's the very "hert o' corn".
Unknown

Conversations were purely parochial, centring round ploughing, sheep shearing, dairying, sewing, reaping, and the events of the parish, national matters, education, and national matters, with education and religion receiving little more than a passing remark.

The district ploughing match was the event of the season when ploughmen, speaking encouragingly and soothingly to gaily groomed horses, strove with great earnestness to gain the coveted silver cup. No one who could miss the match, and children who did not play truant were snubbed by the venturesome enthusiasts who went to the match and accepted their severe punishment the next day in the spirit that the day's enjoyment was worth it.

At nightfall, long after sunset in wintertime, the tired workers wended their homeward-weary way to their thatched *butt-and-ben* [two-room cottage], miserable houses called "hame", where the guid wife, if not working in the fields, had perforce to work hard, looking after the weans, attending to the poultry and probably a pig, keeping a' things snod, and preparing the food. Burns writes:

At length his lonely cot appears in view,
Beneath the shelter of an aged tree;
Th' expectant wee-things, toddlin, stacher through
To meet their dad, wi flichterin noise and glee.
The Cotter's Saturday Night
Robert Burns (1786)

After the simple evening meal of porridge and milk, scones and oatmeal cakes, an egg or two, and maybe, if times were good, cheese or bacon, with the kettle singing merrily on the swey, the family settled down for the evening, the cat purring on the home-made rug before the wide-open hearth, father reading the local newspaper, mother busy making "aul claes [clothes] look amaist as gude as new", with the children sitting around the fire in a semi-circle chatting, laughing, playing draughts, dominoes, or other games, and squabbling. Amid all this, homework had to be attended to, much of it being memorising work.

Clothes and clogs passed down the family line until they refused to hold together any longer, and schoolbooks were treasured, read, and re-read until they fell to pieces.

Such was the homely, hard-rustic life in the fields and the home of the agricultural peasants in which I shared with growing resentment for however romantic butt-and-bens are, I was always conscious of being cramped and held down by hard, soulless economic laws framed to serve the well-to-do and without consideration for the less fortunate, but in every way better, people who were rich in their families and honest towards all.

In and around the "aul hoose" the consciousness gradually broke in on me that I was a human entity, a living soul able to soar above and going beyond the hard circumstances in which I found myself, in the centre of a large, beautiful, good family of boys and girls with whom I played, laughed, and quarrelled, but ever loved intensely with my whole heart and soul.

Humanely speaking the circumstances in which I found myself, coupled with the human environment, could lead only to a life of slavery in the fields from which, if I had allowed myself to be drawn into such a life, there was practically no possibility of breaking away.

Fortunately, there was that within me which caused me to loathe the life of an agricultural labourer, and everything connected therewith, which earned for me the displeasure of the farmers and the ridicule of my fellow beings, who looked upon me, and rightly so, as not being none of them.

The opening of the prison doors by an angel to allow St. Peter to pass to freedom and to escape death was no more miraculous than the opening up of the way for me to escape from farm slavery to Glasgow where I became a railwayman and met my "Angel".

I loved the country, with its woods and glens, river and burn [watercourse], flowers, birds, trees, and the smell of new-mown hay, the sound of the reaper in the harvest field, and to see the coarseness of farm life, the unsatisfiable inexorable incessant demands of the farmers, and the hapless plight of the humble, honest, blythe peasant folk appalled me. From tender years, I dreamed of the day when I could throw over my beloved countryside for the drab, dull life of the city, where life would be freer, and opportunities would present themselves for advancement in social and financial spheres.

I thought of Canada and the United States, but far-away, darkest Africa only crystallised in my dream-thoughts during the Boer war (1899-1902).

THE AUL' HOOSE:
"ROUCAN COTTAGE"

Near the road through the moss, wi' its heather and pest,
Where the road meets the brae, on the hill rises steep,
Stans' a sma' theekit hoose, wi' a wee butt-and-ben,
To the bairnies a ha' like the hoose in t' glen.

Snodly snug was t hoose, wi' a rose on its wa'
Wi' the weans cuddlin' doen, when the wun drave the sna
In the moss on the linn, on ower the green braes
An the laddies ran barefit, an tore a' their claes.

On the brae near the mill, lads an lassies made een,
'en richt hartsom thy danced, an played on the green.
Weel kant were the nests, a' ower the hale lan'
In the Kirk they sang praises, a tunefu' aul' psalm.

The Kirkyaird is upby, an skulefreens are noo there,
The lads an the lassies, whae danced at the fair.
The dithery aul' castle, an the Kirk wi' the bell,
Of sair fechtin' lang syn, an great preachers cud tell.

We loe the wee hoose, near the burn on the brae,
For its freenship 'n lagter, gey aften we're wae
Wi' t' ingle nook snod, an t' wag o' t' wa'
Tae the wanderers aye hame, be they in cottage, or ha'.

J.R.

Roucan:
Aul Hoose Reimagined

The road by the bog, where heather grows deep,
Winds up a hill beside a path in fine upkeep,
To our thatched haven with enough room within,
A cozy shelter, that house in the glen.
Snug within its walls covered in roses so fair,
We snuggled away from the bite of frosty air.
Through bogs and streams we freely strayed
Playing in muddy clothes worn out and frayed.
By the mill we danced, as sheep grazed near,
Barefoot on swaying grass, free of all fear.
Birds came to nest from all over the land,
Drawn by psalms sung with hearts and hands.
Near the schoolyard my friends and I stayed,
chasing after lambs, we endlessly played.
The shivering castle, once a refuge from strife,
The church with old bells, that sanctuary of life.
I adored our abode, near the streams and slopes,
While my parents kindled all dreams and hopes.
I was always kept warm by the hearth in the wall,
how I loved that place. It was my home, my all.

Ruarri Mackenzie Rogan, 1996.
Grahamstown.

Roucan Cottage

Mrs. J. Rogan, with Harold and Douglas

Chapter 1
The Roucan

I consider myself one of many boys growing up in rural Scotland in the late 1800s who could not have foreseen the tremendous change and horror that would unfold in the decades ahead. But, looking back on those hard, cold Scottish years, I have a newfound appreciation for the past. As I reflect on all that happened after I left the mists of my childhood in Scotland, passed through the Cape of Storms into the Cape of Good Hope, and first saw the majestic Table Mountain shrouded in mist, I am filled with a sense of nostalgia. In the twilight of my life, I strive to pass on my experiences, reflections, and wisdom to future generations, so that they can understand the hardships of the past, appreciate the present, and face the challenges of the future with courage and poise.

I was born in Kinning Park District, Glasgow, on the 29th of March 1881, when Winter would be going out like a lion and Spring coming in like a lamb. During March, the wind blows cold and shrilly round the Bens, through the glens, and along the bleak town streets, where the beautifully dressed, brilliantly lit shop windows gave a measure of comfort to the people whose business and work demanded their braving all weathers.

At the time, the distant Boer War stirred up concern and unease, even in Scotland. The conflict raged far away in Africa. Yet, even in Glasgow, its impact was felt. People talked about the news that, in February 1881, just before my birth, General Sir George Colley and over 200 of his men were defeated by General Piet Joubert's forces on Majuba Hill in South Africa's Natal region. Despite the vast distance between Scotland and South Africa, I was born into one world and came of age in the other.

I was the sixth child in a family of thirteen, nine of whom survived infancy. Eight are still alive in 1949, living in Scotland, England, Canada, and South Africa. One sister now in England spent time in India.

After my birth, my father left his nine-year tenure at a railway company and returned to his birthplace in Roucan, shaping me into a country lad by destiny. Reflecting on this decision, I now believe there was divine intervention at play, though at the time, I had no religion in my heart and would have dismissed such thoughts as mere superstition, more fitting for Catholics than practical Scotsmen. That said, time has opened my mind to the possibility of wonder, and I can only see the intricate dance of fate that unfolded as nothing short of magical.

While my father left the railway behind, my future father-in-law, Mr. Smith, was climbing the ranks, eventually securing a promotion to Station Master in Glasgow. This simultaneous departure and ascent set the stage for a young man from the country to find himself in the elevated company of his lifelong love. The serendipitous encounter with Mr. Smith's daughter, my wife, whom I affectionately call "My Angel", was a heavenly appointment.

Had I not grown up as a country lad from Dumfriesshire, I would never have been sent to Maxwell Park Station, nor would I have secured a position with the Caledonian Railway. And without those crucial pieces falling into place, I would not have met the love of my life.

While my father sought to find his footing in country life, our family briefly stayed in Roucan before moving to the picturesque farm of "Fernie Cleugh", named after the fern-filled glen. At the age of four, I began attending the parish school in the village of Torthorwald, three miles away. Part of Torthowald law was that it was the home of John G. Paton, the renowned South Seas Missionary. Children clung to every word of the tales of Paton's heroism, resilience, and prayerful patience amid cannibals and ceaseless warfare.

The modest dwelling in Torthorwald where Paton spent his childhood attracted many tourists annually from all corners of the globe. His fame had spread throughout the English-speaking world, drawing visitors to the site of his upbringing. But in his later years, Paton returned to Torthorwald as an unassuming, white-bearded man, unrecognised and uncelebrated. As the saying goes, a prophet is not without honour, save in his own country.

Subsequently, our family relocated to a wind-swept cottage encircled by mist-shrouded hills and expansive meadows where foxes prowled, wild game roamed, and rabbits darted about. The eerie silence was punctuated only by the haunting cry of the curlew overhead. The desolate landscape took a toll on our family's health, and tragically, we lost one of our own, diminishing our family's number by one. Such losses were not uncommon in those days, and our family bore the grief of losing a sibling and a young child with stoicism, pressing forward as best we could.

Continuing our slow progress as we tried to find a place in the world, in 1887, the family moved to Tinwald Downs. Though close to one another in proximity, the two places differed greatly in character and atmosphere. Tinwald was a sooty industrial place with coal mines, factories, a stench of sulphur, and the constant hum of machinery. Roucan, on the other hand, was a tranquil hamlet surrounded by misty hills and land that you could live off.

I remember the day we attended the Queen Victoria's 50th Jubilee celebration in Tinwald. Bonfires were burning on each parish's highest hill, and there were people everywhere, some celebrating, some grudgingly honouring the monarchy. The economy had taken its toll on many families, with children leaving home and people migrating to Canada and Australia. Men joined the police force and railways, while young women travelled to nurse the men who gave their flesh for a soldier's wage in any of the many land battles around the globe.

Even in Tinwald, we still called Roucan our home. None of us had any love for the coal mines. So when the opportunity to return to Roucan in 1889 presented itself, our family was more than eager. Mother was especially overjoyed to be back in the place she loved. We arrived at "Roucan Cottage", which is still inhabited today by a married minister. I have since found out that the thatch roof of the cottage was replaced with a slate roof, a modernism that erased centuries of tradition. Eventually, our family dispersed and Mother, having fulfilled her dream, passed away in the cottage in 1915. Father followed her in 1934.

Goldsmith could have written of the Roucan:

Sweet Auburn, loveliest village of the plain,
Where health and plenty cheer'd the labouring swain,
Where smiling Spring its earliest visit paid,
And parting summer's lingering blooms delayed…
Oliver Goldsmith (1770)

As far as is known, no notable figures or poets from Roucan have written about the area specifically. Even still, the Dumfries and Galloway region of Scotland, where Roucan is located, has no doubt inspired many artists and writers over the years. The Scottish poet Robert Burns resided in nearby Dumfries and his work is steeped in the beauty and culture of the region. Other authors such as Sir Walter Scott and J.M. Barrie were also inspired by the Dumfries and Galloway area.

I loved the Roucan with all the loveable intensity of a child, and all my daydreams were woven round the place and district. Secretly, I pitied the other children who had not the privilege of living in our hamlet, and I now see they must have been sorry for me for living in such a place. There was to me no place comparable with the Roucan, and my surprise was great when on starting work in Dumfries, 3½ miles distant, I met people who, unbelievably, had never heard of the place.

My graphic descriptions of its dreamy, old-time beauty and its place in the history of Scotland to my chagrin were received with an incredulous smile and mostly cold disinterestedness. As my horizon widened, I found that most people had only a hazy idea of Scotland's geographical position, connecting it with Aberdeen, looking upon the land as somewhere near to the North Pole where everybody ate porridge, danced to the Highland Fling, and played the bagpipes, not to mention Scotch whiskey and kilts.

Everything in and around the Roucan was old. Thatched cottages with large, wide, open hearths, walls built with a sort of "dagga" [earthen or adobe plaster], crumbling with the years, old wells from which the people drew their water, horse-drawn circular grinding mills, the scythe, sickle, and heavy ploughs. Women dressed during the week in shirt, heavy skirts and on the Sabbath, long black dresses, with a small bonnet (the smaller, the more fashionable) were in vogue. Only the children moved quickly whilst the men wore heavy tweed clothes, heavy boots, or clogs, for the lands and leather leggings. But beneath the rough exterior, there beat an honest, upright, humble heart attuned to the joys, sorrows, and struggles common to all the peasants.

The new reaping machine, now entirely outmoded, was gradually ousting the scythe, a single telephone wire passed overhead, the "Boneshaker", the forerunner of the bicycle, and the stagecoach, a much beloved means of travel, was still fresh in the memories of our parents. Its disappearance from the King's Highway was viewed with much regret by the older generation who loved to hear the winding horn, to watch the swift gallop of the steaming four-in hand over the badly pitted, rutted, potholed country road, the fast travel by railway still holding terrors for the slow-moving old folks.

The Roucan, in my day, consisted of about a dozen cottages, mostly with thatch roofs, but in my father's boyhood it was a large place inhabited by agricultural peasants, cloggers, and a blacksmith, with weaving as a well-established industry. The first blow fell when the Lairds [lords/gentry] decided to amalgamate the small farms without regard to human suffering, thus depriving much of the community of their means of livelihood. Unfortunately, on top of this calamity, the hand-weaving loom was outdated and outmoded by the introduction of the power-drive loom, and weavers, a fine, industrious, home-loving body of men, found themselves stranded beside their cumbersome contraptions not knowing whither to turn.

Old people, unable to migrate, slowly pined away in soul-destroying destitution, whilst not a few had perforce to seek refuge within the inhospitable, inhuman walls of the poorhouse, from where there was no return. Young men and women emigrated to Canada and Australia, men joined the police force and railways, whilst not a few joined the army, fighting in many lands and battles.

Such was Scotland's gratitude towards her own people in the days of "Good Queen Victoria" and the inhumanity of Lairds and others to men and women who had slaved from childhood years for a wage altogether insufficient to keep body and soul together in reasonable comfort, let alone providing for sickness, old age, or unforeseen contingencies.

As a child I met some of these old people who, in almost every instance, had never been more than twenty to thirty away from their home. They had never seen a ship. Never travelled by train.

The church smiled benignly on the Lairds, who, encouraged by Toryism, spent their leisure (which seemed to embrace most of the year) holidaying in distant parts, foxhunting, attending "hunt" balls, and generally, in their own estimation, having a good time without giving a thought to their unfortunate peasants or to the many workless and beggars who fell by the way.

The iniquity of the order of things burned itself deeply into my youthful soul and I rebelled with my whole heart against the economic tyranny that held the land in its merciless grip.

Once, I talked with a one-legged veteran of the Crimean War (1854) who had been reduced to a state of destitution on a country's grateful pension of 6d. [6 pennies] per day whilst the sons of the well-to-do lived in lavish, extravagant luxury, coupled with idleness.

Everyone was nominally connected with the Established Church (there was no other in the district), but what spiritual fellowship could there be in a church where the landowners looked on their servants with haughty contempt, and where the Minister, following their lead, favoured the farmers and well-to-do, and gave only a distant nod to the less fortunate, but better men and women.

Roucanites were true sons of the soil: robust, strong-as-a-horse men with their faces hid behind untrimmed beards (even the boys looked forward to the day when they would also grow a beard), unkempt, shaggy hair, hard-worked, horny hands, slightly stooping, broad shoulders, muscular arms, who walked with a long, slow, heavy step. The Townsmen called them "clodhoppers" and made sport of their coarse, not unusually mud-stained, heavy clothes and iron-shod clogs, which were out of place in the cobbled streets in the town.

What though on hamely fare we dine,
Wear hoddin' grey, an' a' that;
Gie fools their silks, and knaves their wine;
A Man's a Man for a' that
A Man's A Man For A' That
Robert Burns (1795)

Children were perforce reared haphazardly, without any refinements or reasonable comforts, dressing and caring for themselves from an early age, washing in a nearby burn, and eating wholesome porridge with milk, potatoes, vegetables, and eggs, or an occasional rabbit for stew. We ate freely of sloes [fruit of the Blackthorn *Prunus spinosa*], bramble, hazel nuts, wild cherries, wild crab-apples, chestnuts, young turnips, and nothing came amiss that was edible. Dieting of children or grownups was unknown and evidently unnecessary, and it was good that such was the case seeing the nearest doctor was 3½ miles distant, and he only responded to a call in the case of an apparent grievous sickness.

Toys were unknown except for rag dolls for the girls and "bools" (marbles) for boys, and as there was no organised sport, children followed their own free bent in groups.

We ran about the braes,
And we gethered hips en slaes,
And we tore a' oer claes
And were late for the skule in the morning
Old Roucan Song

During the summer, after working gruelling 12-hour shifts in the fields, the men in the community would often play a game of quoits, or horseshoes, while in the winter they would switch to carpet bowls or "bools", which was popular throughout the country. But it was during the colder months that they really shone, playing the "Roarin' game of Curling" on the ice, where both gentry and peasant alike would call each other by their Christian names and slap each other on the back. It was a rare occasion where the social and spiritual divide between the classes was briefly bridged. Another such occasion was the Annual Ploughing Match.

Still, Christmas was practically unknown in the area and not celebrated as a season of worship and commemoration of the birth of Jesus. Instead, it was the New Year that was widely celebrated, with the men passing around bottles and getting drunk, much to the disapproval of the almost entirely teetotaling women.

As for transportation, the peasants had no vehicles of their own and relied on horse-drawn scotchcarts ---gigs (two wheels) and phaetons (four wheels) --- and the occasional char-a-banc [touring coach], while these modes of transportation were more commonly used by the higher social strata of the community.

WINTER IN SCOTLAND

The howling storm drave through the glen,
En ower each sna' capped lofty Ben,
The burnies fu' louped ower the Stanes
En' sna' lay deep aroun' the Hames.

Frae oot the North blew frozen sleet,
En fog hung low ower murky street
Frae mornin' oor, tae dark at een,
Through lowering cloud nae sun was seen

Deep in the glen the sna' draps lay,
En a' was deed till Springtime ray
Birds refuge foun' in tree an hedge
An Sheep were seen near sheltering ledge.

Let Northwun' blow ower Ben tops high
The Lord O' a' is ever nigh,
He gaes us strength an wondrous grace
To live through a' an seek His face.
J. R. (19 October 1947)

WINTER

The wintry West extends his blast,
    The hail and rain does blaw,
Or, the stormy North sends driving forth
    The blinding sleet and snaw.
While, tumbling brown, the burn comes down
    And roars frae bank tae brae
And bird and beast in covert rest
    And pass the heartless day.
J. R.

Behold! The grateful hearts doth rise,
To Him who paints the cosmic skies,
The Architect of land and sea,
Whose design weaves all, both you and me.

The Earth, a canvas, floating free,
With dancing waters, wild and free,
The orbs that twinkle bright and clear,
guide us on our path without fear.

We tread the path of His design,
Through shadowed lands and light divine,
In Scottish grace, our tartan wove,
Our steps aligned, His love bestrode.

J. R.
Durban, 15 June 1941

In me, beauty doth reside,
And lofty thoughts, doth guide,
With morning's sun, shining bright,
Inspiration doth take flight.

J. R.
Durban, 15 June 1941

In Him, I find the light and path,
My spirit filled with peace and faith.
With Him, I walk, in converse still,
leaving woes and sins behind at will.
Each day with Him, my life enshrined,
Guided by His love, my heart aligned.

J. R.
Johannesburg, 5 April 1946

Chapter 2
Work During School Years

Work, for the night is coming,
Work through the morning hours,
Work while the dew is sparkling,
Work 'mid springtime flowers,
Work while the day grows brighter
Under the glowing sun,
Work, for the night is coming
When man's work is done.
Hymn No. 261
The Church Hymnary (1902)

Travelling from the Sunday School picnic in scotchcarts loaned for the occasion, the hymn "Work, for the night is coming" was chosen for community singing, aptly expressing the spirit of the district where work eclipsed all else, even refreshment of body and soul. Commencing in the "sparkling dew", through rain and in shine, there was no cessation until the shades of night were cast over the land.

In the hurry to keep pace with the seasons, children were brutishly pressed into service by firmly established economic slavery, and in the fields, they hoed turnips, assisted in the harvest fields, and worked as required with aching shoulders and not a little resentment.

I was not lazy, being eager to help augment the family income, but from early years, I detested the coarseness of the conversations of the men and women, the vulgarity that continued uninterruptedly throughout the day, and the unfairness of my having to work hard under such vile conditions. But work I had to — the tiredness, weariness, and bodily pain were mine, and must be borne alone and without sympathy from anyone.

The following record of a few instances of employment on which I was engaged gives a fair general idea of the farm duties which fell to my lot:

Shoo-ing Crows:

My first employment, when about 10 years old, was to "shoo crows" on a large, huge for a small boy, field of young turnips for the princely sum of 2/6d. [2 shillings and 6 pennies] per week, or about ½d (one halfpenny) per hour.

Crows are notoriously early risers, beating the sun to ensure their catching the early worm, and consequently I needed to beat them at their own game by being in the field, some distance from home, no later than 3 a.m., seven days weekly , for, sad to relate, crows do not respect the scotch sabbath.

The "shoo-ing" was by no means a sinecure, especially for one so young, and between my keeping a watchful eye on the farmer, who from time to time appeared suddenly out of the morning haze, and chasing after the crows, soon I was thoroughly exhausted, my condition being aggravated by the fact of my having had no breakfast.

Hungry crows are persistent creatures, and as I "shoo-ed" them from one spot in the field they flew with loud caws, caws, to another part and commenced immediate operations on the young turnips, which they rooted up to get at the worms.

I had to run hither and thither as quickly as possible over the rough-ploughed land (generally rain-sodden) for several hours on end, and by the time the well-fed crows, to the chagrin of the farmers and my disgust, decided to fly to their rookeries, I was in much need of breakfast (notwithstanding that I had assisted the crows by eating a turnip or two myself), a wash in the burn, and a rest before going to school.

Hoeing Turnips:

Have you ever hoed turnips, or anything else sown in long, long furrows? I do not mean a cabbage patch or flower bed, but furrows half a mile or so long, consisting of heavy loam soil, weeds, and stones, where immediately one furrow was finished there were ever so many more waiting to be hoed as quickly as possible.

Twelve hours daily, 72 hours weekly, for 3/6d [3 s. and 6 p.] per week with aching shoulders, limbs threatening to double up and collapse any minute, the frail body feeling as though it was falling to pieces, with a splitting headache. But the turnips had to be hoed as quickly and cheaply as possible, and I, abused, threatened, and sick at heart, drew upon every ounce of my childish strength to keep pace with strong, muscular, men and women, with frames of iron, whilst able-bodied men pleaded for work, or loafed in the towns at street corners.

Childish tears, open revolt, and the cry of anguish called forth no sympathetic word or expression of kindness from the soil-hardened men and women, and lagging behind through sheer inability to exert more strength only called forth accusations of laziness.

The Threshing Machine:

Probably the most exacting and strenuous task which ever fell to my lot in my tender years was the difficult work of loosening sheaves of corn on the top of a power-driven threshing machine.

Dust filled the air, causing me to become half-blinded and parched with thirst, the large drum revolved with a deafening "hum" and sheaves were forked at top speed from the ground to the platform on which I was standing. My work was to loosen and hand them to the operator feeding the mill. Stop, I dare not, otherwise I would have been buried by the constantly oncoming sheaves and the language of the operator would have frightened me. Half-dazed faint and exhausted, I had to carry on without respite for 12 hours daily with a break of one hour only.

Carrying Trees:

Carrying baskets filled with young trees intended for planting far up the hillside was hard work and much too heavy for a child of my years, but I was buoyed with the knowledge that I was helping the family exchequer.

My slender frame was very much overtaxed, but as haste was not required, and I had been asked to undertake heavier duties, I was satisfied with my endeavour to do a man's work for a child's wage — 3/- [3s.] per week.

Funeral Notices:

Going from door to door over the widely scattered district to deliver the verbal news of a death was not work, yet it had to be done without telephones or a postal service and with only a weekly paper.

A lad was selected to go the round of the isolated farms and cottages, advising the dwellers of the passing of one who was known to them all, and one time, the bereaved family, to my chagrin, selected me for the solemn task.

I was carefully instructed in the use of "correct" English, the homely dialect being considered unsuitable for such an occasion, and so I set out on my long journey delivering at the widely separated dwellings a mixed-up message in the following terms:

"A' heve to tell you that Tibby Le-e (illegible) de-ed last nicht, an the funeral will take place the morn's efternane."

The effort required to deliver such an auspicious message was considerable and I was relieved temporarily of my nervous strain as I left each cottage for the next one, generally a mile or two distant.

From early age, I needed to go to Dumfries on errands for my parents and others. At times boys were used to "run to town" to buy a bottle of whiskey for some poor soul who had fallen victim to drink, but I always resolutely refused to go on such errands.

Water had to be carried from the well, wood chopped, dishes washed, and the baby nursed, and whilst I did my share of the domestic work, I was never a willing worker. Somehow or other I did not just fit in, and the work in the household was not congenial to me.

Railwayman

In fair Dumfries, where dreams took flight,
A youth aspired to reach new heights.
From verdant fields to shops of trade,
His spirit restless, unafraid.

Amid the joy of annual fairs,
A deeper yearning stirred his cares.
Through stormy nights and trials dire,
He sought a life that would inspire.

A clerk he was, but dreams did swell,
For railways called with magic spell.
In Glasgow, the Caledonian Line,
A destiny, a plan divine.

Through trials, temptations, he endured,
An angel's love, his heart secured.
With guiding hand and steadfast grace,
His journey led to love's embrace.

Ascending high the railway's crest,
In work and faith, he found his quest.
With praise and honours by his side,
To greater heights, he'd ever glide.

In Glasgow's heart, a railwayman,
He met his love, life's sweetest plan.
With fate's guidance, firm and sure,
He found a life, both rich and pure.

Ruarri Mackenzie Rogan, 1996.
Grahamstown.

Chapter 3
DUMFRIES

"The Queen of the South"

1896–1898

O' a' the toons in Scotland, there's nane can beat
Dumfries;
Tis nestled here in beauty's garb, in cleanliness and
peace;
The sichts within an' roon the toon, are really
something gran'
The centre o' attraction, tae every foreign lan'.
Unknown

The river Nith, separating Dumfries from Maxwelltown, flowed through the town on its way to the Solway Firth. It was in Dumfries that Robert the Bruce slew the traitor Comyn at the alter of Gray Friars Church in 1306. Robert Burns, the Scottish National Poet whose beautiful monument stands in Church Crescent, is buried in St. Michael's Church Yard, and the house where he died is visited by thousands of his admirers from all parts of the world annually.

The town was my constant wonder, with its shops and (to my childish mind) endless streets and traffic. The annual Fair was the centre of attraction with its merry-go-rounds, shooting galleries, hobbyhorses, and side-shows, when from far and near the peasants, released from toil for one day, thronged the town in their thousands, spending, in many cases, their last penny in frivolous enjoyment.

Children looked forward to the day with eager anticipation, more so than to the Annual Sunday School picnic, and joyfully walked, literally ran, several miles or more to town to quickly spend their pocket money of about three pennies (one ticket).

The fair was held right after the harvest, when everyone was in jovial mood, and the few extra shillings they had been able to earn were quickly and foolishly squandered, although they were sorely needed in the home.

Replying to an advertisement which appeared in the "Dumfries Standard", I was successful in obtaining an appointment as junior clerk in a fairly large Draper-Dressmaking establishment, near Burns' Monument at a commencing wage of 5/- [5s.] per week, gladly turning my back on farm labour and "life in the country" in the hope that the appointment would lead me further and farther away from the hated life on the lands.

Clad in a new suit with long trousers, wearing a collar and tie, and boots instead of clogs, I endeavoured to be a thorough little man in my congenial new circumstances where I was ever so happy.

I continued to live at the Roucan, enjoying the one hour's walk each way in the summer and autumn, when the lark sang high in the air, the call of the cuckoo floated sweetly through the air and the road was bordered with wildflowers and heather. The air was redolent of the fragrance of new-mown hay, with the glory of the Lord over the beautiful land. But the winter and early spring months — they were a nightmare, with lashing rain, and cold, benumbing sleet, frost, and snow (one or the other, always), and as I trudged along the slippery road with its ruts and mudholes, leaning against the bitter, strong North gale in dense darkness, I had to keep a tight grip of myself to prevent panicking.

No one ever took the journey without a very good reason for doing so, and most people hesitated before taking it at all, which, in the winter, was an adventure. As a rule, I had the road to myself, with no landmarks visible in the murky darkness to cheer me on my way. In the eeriness, coupled with my nervous tension, the sudden hoot of an owl, or the stealthy step of a poacher who could not be seen in the darkness, made the pulse beat quicker, and the high-pitched howling wind blowing through the trees worked adversely on the nervous system, demanding my drawing upon every ounce of my childish courage to enable me to sustain the ordeal. But I never admitted to anyone that I was nervous, being afraid to do so, facing the fearful ordeal and winning through.

When bending to the storm on dark night, I collided face on with a pedestrian walking in the opposite direction, and it is difficult to say who got the greatest fright, although I nearly collapsed from it.

Only a country lad used to the vigours of the severe weather on the land, and the terrors to a lad, of the darkness could have stood the mental and physical strain on that lonely, dark, ghost-accredited road, typically drenched to the skin, covered with frozen-sleety snow, walking dangerously on the ice-covered road.

After about a year, the firm with which I was employed changed hands, and very soon after, I obtained employment with a firm of wholesale groceries at a wage of 7/6d. [7s. 6p.] per week, but since starting work in the town, a firm determination to become a railwayman, if at all possible, had gradually taken hold of me. Although I was not in touch with a Railway System or Railway servants, the red glare from the engine fire-box on the low-lying clouds of the night express to London, as I tramped homewards in the dense darkness, gave to me a deep sense of spiritual fellowship and the firm assurance came to me that one day I would be in the service of one of the Railway Companies.

The guidance and intervention of my Heavenly Father in the affairs of my life at this time can now be discerned, under whose loving care I made application for appointment to the Caledonian Railway Company in Glasgow, although that Company was practically unknown in and around Dumfries. Herein is revealed His loving wisdom, for had I applied to the Glasgow and South Western Company, which logically speaking I should have done seeing it was the Railway Company serving Dumfries, I could not have been appointed to Maxwell Park where I met "My Angel".

Thus God was preparing me to travel "His Way", under the protection of His unseen guardian angel via Dumfries to Glasgow where I started to live a life of freedom and where I met and loved immediately my beautiful, sweet Peggy, and from there to South Africa with the avowed intention of preparing the way to make a home for my own sweet darling. But it was first necessary that I should be prepared in the crucible of hard circumstances, fearful temptation, and severe, gruelling, but congenial work, to fit me for the greater work and increased responsibilities which lay far ahead.

I did not know the Lord at this time and was not conscious of His guiding presence in my life, nor ever dreamed that He was leading me step by step to Maxwell Park where meeting with Peggy — My Angel — my whole outlook in life was to be immediately and miraculously changed for the better.

I do not wish to convey the impression that God singled me out for special favour above my fellowmen, but I do believe that he planned my path and set the course of my future career and marriage, and I, unconsciously willing, was found in the way — His way. Such opportunities come, I believe, to everyone at or near the beginning of life's journey, and if the open door is courageously entered with honesty of purpose, stepways to advancement are found in hard work and conscientious endeavour.

Such has been my experience in my gradual climb to the top of the Railway ladder.

My first certificate of character:

> B. Dickson, Dressmaking, Silks, dresses, millinery
> and mantles

Church Crescent,

DUMFRIES.

I have pleasure in stating that John Rogan has been with me as an apprentice clerk for the last year. I have found him a very attentive and industrious lad, very willing and obliging. His abilities are above the average for his age. His manner is most agreeable.

During the time he has been with us, he has had every opportunity of gaining a knowledge of office work, an opportunity I feel sure he has availed himself of.

He is anxious that he may find a wider sphere so that promotion may be more certain. I can with every confidence recommend him to any party requiring his services. He carries with him my best wishes for his future success in life.

(Sgd.) C.M. WHITE.

Manager

Second Certificate:

C.E. Leader, Dressmaker, Silks, Dresses, Millinery, and Mantles

----

Church Crescent,

DUMFRIES.

5 May 1898

Gentlemen,

The bearer (Mr. John Rogan) was apprenticed with my Predecessor (Miss Dickson) whose books he kept for about six months, also mine for about nine months.

I found him exceedingly accurate, and careful with figures, neat and clean in the books, very industrious and assiduous in his work, and very anxious to make progress. I should not have parted with him, but for the fact of my doing my own bookkeeping.

He is thoroughly trustworthy and honest.

Yours faithfully,

(Sgd.) C. E. LEADER

Third and last Certificate:

This is to certify that John Rogan, Torthorwald, has been in our office, temporary, at different times and we have always found him a thoroughly reliable lad. He is a very careful and efficient clerk for his age, and we can recommend him very highly. His parents, who are known to us, are very respectable people.

(Sgd.) MACGREGOR & COLVERT

I was restless and vaguely dissatisfied with myself and yearned for greater opportunity to improve myself mentally, and in matter of getting an appointment that offered that offered a career. The future as far as I could see held no prospects for me of advancement in Dumfries, where there must have been many avenues along which I could have advanced had I been so inclined, but my eyes were on Glasgow, being determined to become a railwayman, and it is easy to understand that I did not wholeheartedly apply myself to the work at hand, although I was extremely conscientious.

Gradually, I became more and more estranged from the Roucan, my school companions faded out of my life, and the crude coarseness of country life repelled me more than ever.

Chapter 4
Glasgow

1898–1902

Does the road wind up-hill all the way?
Yes, to the very end.
Will the day's journey take the whole long day?
From morn to night, my friend.
Christina Rossetti *Up-Hill* (1861)

When the one-armed country postman delivered a letter from the Caledonian Railway District Headquarters in Glasgow, offering me an appointment if I was considered suitable, I was delirious with joy and trembled with excitement. Realised expectation let loose in a flood of joy overwhelmed me, and I was so eager to be a railwayman that in an hour or two I was on the way to Dumfries Station wearing my entire wardrobe and with 2/- [2s.] in my pocket. A healthy, if somewhat frail lad, abounding in optimism with a zealousness for congenial work, but not on a farm, and a clear conception of right and wrong as they affected my own life.

Mother (my father had left for work) when saying goodbye, asked me never to touch strong drink nor to join the Free Masons, and both requests have been faithfully kept. I have never indulged in any of the so-called "friendly" vices, such as drinking intoxicating liquors, smoking, gambling, and card playing, and at all times I have shunned the use of foul and obscene language, God having filled my mouth, after my conversion with His praise. Under His protecting care, before I gave my heart to Jesus, He kept me pure at a time when many voices were calling me to travel along the broad way which leadeth to destruction.

On that beautiful Spring morning, the Angel of the Lord was very, very near to me as I walked along the lovely, lonely Solway Moss road on my way to Dumfries, which Angel had preserved me from certain death when huge falling stones in the ruins of Torthorwald castle grazed my body some years previously, and who was no leading me unerringly and lovingly to a life of usefulness for my blessed Master in South Africa.

On arrival in Glasgow, the Angel of the Lord, having completed its appointed task, handed me over to "My Angel" Peggy (I mean this absolutely literally), whose sweet, loving influence during my five years residence in Glasgow imparted to me the strength and determination to overcome and live victoriously through many fierce temptations, when without church influences, Christian fellowship, or a knowledge of the way of Salvation, I withstood the onslaughts of Satan, such as humanely speaking, were beyond the powers of human endurance. Bless the Lord, Oh my soul, and all that is within me, give glory unto His Name.

Never to me had the countryside looked so beautiful as on that perfect spring morning when, walking with buoyant, boyish step, I headed for Dumfries Station to commence my second, or possibly third Railway journey. The deep green of the meadows, the heather-decked moss decorated with wildflowers of many hues, the sweet song of the ascending lark, the call of the cuckoo, lambs frolicking in the fields, the smell of new-mown hay, and the song of the workers combined in presenting a picture of spiritual beauty interwoven with the praise of Nature to its Creator, which held me in tune with my Heavenly Father.

Memories of the Roucan were quickly effaced by the glamour of the new life on which I had so optimistically entered, commencing with the scenes of activity and natural beauty I saw in the countryside through which the train sped at high speed.

It all appeared to me as a dream, and I almost dreaded that I would awake to find it was so, until bewildered and dazed, I alighted in Glasgow Central Station uncertain which way to turn. The huge, crowded, busy station, the crowds hurrying to and fro, engines, trains, and bridges of signals bordered on the terrifying, and the unusual din of the city created in me a feeling of lostness and loneliness such as I had never felt when alone in the fields and glens, but there was no desire to return to the Roucan and I was never homesick.

Afraid to break into my precious 2/- with no luggage and no thought of partaking of food, although it was now late afternoon, I cautiously enquired my way along endless busy streets (the carfare would have been 2d. [twopence]) bounded by row upon row of dingy (that is, outwardly), tall tenements that were entered through a "close", with shops on the street level, and a public house not infrequently near to a church at almost every corner, to the residence of my uncle and aunt, where I was received with great friendliness coupled with not a little surprise.

A constant stream of horse=drawn trains passed to and fro with loud clanging bells, and I was particularly interested in the well-fed, beautifully groomed horses, Dumfries being one of the markets of supply for horses.

Railways passed overhead and underneath, Railwaymen in uniform were as common as police officers, and the latter gentlemen were all very courteous and helpful to me as I blindly enquired my way along and through the bewildering maize of streets.

The Staff Superintendent in the Caledonian Railway District offices, scarcely able to see me on the other side of the large, high, square counter, remarked as I presented his letter, to me, "my, ye're awfu' sma'" and after a pause, during which I firmly believe the Holy Spirit of God intervened on my behalf, he added as if speaking to himself, "but a' think ye'll dae". In that fateful moment, my career was decided, and I was duly appointed "Clerk and Porter" on the staff of the Caledonian Railway at a commencing salary of 10/- per week on what was to me the best railway, the "True-to-Time Line" the "Caledonian".

It was all too wonderful — my dream — my greatest yearning was now an accomplished fact, and my career was set. I was a railwayman with the future in my own hands, and my one desire was to prove myself worthy of the appointment.

Praise the Lord, Praise the Lord. Oh, my soul give thanks unto His Holy Name for great and wondrous things hath He done.

Tense with excitement, clad in a green corduroy Caledonian Railway uniform with straight-peaked cap to match and emblazoning "C.R." on the lapels of the jacket and on the cap, I, filled with self-importance and very little else, reported to the Station Master of Maxwell Park, a beautiful suburban station in a fashionable suburb.

Mr Smith received me with Dumfriesshire kindliness, being delighted that I came from the same shire as himself, and I was soon joyously happy, working 12 hours daily, scrubbing floors, cleaning windows, platforms, points, signal lamps, and anything else I could find to rub or scrub. I paid particular attention to the posting of the poster time tables, and Maxwell Park soon gained the reputation of having the neatest display of timetable posters and advertisements. My zealousness for work was unsatiable, and from morning to night I was never idle, but unfortunately this brought me into collision with the other boys who did not share my wholehearted enthusiasm for work first.

On top of scrubbing and bill posting, I had to attend at stated intervals in the small booking office, issuing tickets and assisting in the accounting work, in which I was spoon proficient and received considerable praise for my efficiency and complete understanding of Booking Office routines.

The Spring and Summer months were very enjoyable, whilst late Autumn, Winter, and early Spring were rigorous. It was no picnic rising at 4:30 a.m., straight from bed, (typically facing a blinding storm) taking an hour walk, entering the snow-covered station, lighting signal lamps and fires, sweeping platforms, and attending to the trains all before breakfast. But the thought that life was strenuous never occurred to me — I was a railwayman — I was happy. That when on the late shift, I was 14 hours on duty and had less than 9 hours to myself out of 24 only served to whet my appetite for more work and gave me the joy of keeping more closely in contact with my beloved Railway.

The beat of the engine was music to my ears, giving me a thrill, which lasted until my last journey on the S.A.R. & H. After a gruelling 12-hour shift and an evening meal, I would travel several miles to the Central Station for the express purpose of watching trains come and go and "for the feel" of being part of the great organisation.

My corduroys should have been steeped before wearing, but I did not know this, and no one told me, with the result that on receiving a drenching after a few days wear, I was dyed green from head to foot to the great amusement of my compatriots.

I firmly believed that the working of Maxwell Park Station and the welfare of the travelling community using the station depended to a great extent on my unfailing, efficient, prompt attention to duty, being, in my own estimation at least, an important cog in the organisation of the Caledonian Railway. I worked, lived, and enjoyed life to the full in a spirit of abounding, unquenchable happiness.

Financially, I was solvent, although always bordering on bankruptcy, and although in frequent financial straits I never borrowed money or anything else. Out of my 10/- per week, 8/- were disbursed for board, and with 2/- per week, I clothed and kept myself in boots, and met miscellaneous expenditure, accomplishing the almost impossible, for such it was.

For pleasure, I visited Art Galleries, Museums, and other public places of interest and was never tired exploring the many large, beautiful Parks of which Glasgow was extremely well supplied. They were all free, and to get to them I walked many miles, being unwilling to expend ½d., 1d., or 1½d. on tram fares, Glasgow trams being the cheapest in the world at that time.

A few days after my arrival at Maxwell Park (1898) an incident occurred which altered the whole outlook of my life and gave to me much-needed new direction for the better. Miss Margaret Smith, second daughter of Mr. & Mrs. Smith, of the Station House, asked me my name, and at that moment I knew that Peggy meant more to me than anyone else in the world. I, John Rogan, late of Roucan Village, a shy, awkward country lad who had scarcely ever spoken to, or looked at, a girl, was in love — desperately so. A new force had come into my life, and instinctively I knew that it was for this purpose, God had prepared the way for my appointment to Maxwell Park. It was for this meeting with the girl whom I believed would one day be my wife, that I had addressed my application for appointment to the Caledonian Railway under the guidance of the Holy Spirit, and in order that I should meet my Peggy, the Angel of the Lord intervened when the Staff Superintendent hesitated before he said "But ye'll dae".

A new vital force, love, had come into my life, and I knew even if but vaguely that this girl was my Heaven-chosen life's companion, my one desire being to hear her speak, see her radiant smile, and to be near her, without being able to breathe a word of my love.

My Heavenly Father had indeed been good — I was a railwayman and had met the most beautiful and sweetest girl of all time — My Angel. Thus, I was gloriously happy living on a higher and nobler level than thitherto, a mere boy in the midst of fearful temptation, with no church or social influences, protected, influenced, sweetened, and filled with holy love for my God-appointed Angel.

I began to look forward to the day when I could tell Peggy of my love, but remembering that her father was my Station Master, a much-exalted position in my estimation, and my salary was 10/- per week, only I kept the sacred secret to myself.

> Time doth sweetly, smoothly glide,
> When there's love at home.
> John Hugh McNaughton *Love at Home*

Maxwell Park will ever remain dear to me — around its memory still hangs the joy of work, the kindness of the passengers, the beautiful Park with the lake, military and civil bands playing on the summer evenings and the Station House where kindly Mr. and Mrs. Smith made me welcome, and I adored my Angel in the sweet, loving setting of the family circle.

The Elixer

Teach me, my God and King,
In all things Thee to see,
And what I do in anything
To do it as for Thee.

Not rudely, as a beast,
To run into an action;
But still to make Thee prepossest,
And give it his perfection.

A man that looks on glass,
On it may stay his eye;
Or if he pleaseth, through it pass,
And then the heav'n espy.

All may of Thee partake:
Nothing can be so mean,
Which with his tincture—"for Thy sake"—
Will not grow bright and clean.

A servant with this clause
Makes drudgery divine:
Who sweeps a room as for Thy laws,
Makes that and th' action fine.

This is the famous stone
That turneth all to gold;
For that which God doth touch and own
Cannot for less be told.
George Herbert (1633) *The Temple*
Sacred Poems and Private Ejaculations

Margaret Gillieson Smith

Aged 4 years.

Aged 19 years.

Chapter 5
My Angel

Margaret Gillieson Smith

Born
Dundee, Scotland, 30 September, 1882

"Bonnie" Dundee used to describe itself as Scotland's second commercial city, and was known as the City of Jute, Jams and Journalists.

At the time Peggy was born, Mr. Smith, her father, was a Main Line Railway Guard, having joined the service of the Caledonian Railway in 1870, when Railways were still very much in their infancy. From 1873 until 1892 he was a passenger train guard, and from the latter year until his retirement from the position of Station Master, Maxwell Park Station, Glasgow, during 1920, he occupied the grade of station Master.

On one occasion Mr. Smith was the Assistant Guard on Queen Victoria's special train, when it was en route to or from Balmoral.

Mrs. Smith, a beautiful, accomplished woman, hailed from Inverness, where her parents were much esteemed residents. Her Grandfather who had an extensive shoemaker's business in Inverness, was a prominent Free Mason, with considerable intellectual capacity and literary hobbies. He had a nice turn in the direction of verse and some of his compositions were set by him to music.

It is on record that Mr. MacKenzie in his early days had a phenomenal memory, having been known to correctly repeat 400 different figures which were run off to him by the "Examiner." He was born in 1830 – 15 years after the Battle of Waterloo.

My darling was the third child in a family of seven, who like the Rogan's were all too soon scattered over England, Scotland, South America, India, and South Africa; two girls, Lizzie, the eldest and Peggy, having been selected out of many aspirants for service in the mission field, India.

Peggy received a sound education, acquiring a good knowledge of French and she studied the piano with considerable success. In 1898, the year we met, Peggy had just commenced a business career in a large firm of Ladies Tailors, where she quickly earned the praise of the management for dexterity, zeal, and aptitude, and of the employees for amicability, sweetness of disposition and friendliness.

Peggy was an enthusiastic member of Titwood Parish Church, where under the ministry of the Rev. W.H. Rankine, B.D., she found the Lord at the early age of 16 years, and of the Sunday School, where she shone brightly for Jesus.

In my Darling's diary for August, 1899, the following entries appear indicating a high spiritual state, perfect trust, and complete faith such as is not generally found in one of such tender years:

"I gave my heart to Jesus on Thursday, 20th of April, 1899.
Rules for Daily Life:
Begin the day with God.
Kneel down to him in prayer.
Lift up Thy heart to his abode,
And seek His love to share.

Open the Book of God
And read a portion there;
That it may hallow all thy thoughts
And sweeten all thy care.

Go through the day with God,
Whate'er thy work may be,
Where'er thou art – at home, abroad
He still is near to Thee.

Converse in mind with God,
Thy spiring, heavenward raise;
Acknowledge every good bestowed
And offer grateful praise.

Lie down at night with God,
Who gives His servants sleep,
When thou tread'st the vale of death
He will Thee guard and keep.

None of self and all of Thee

Oh! the bitter shame and sorrow
That a time could ever be,
When I let the Saviour's pity
Plead in vain, and proudly answered
All of self and none of Thee.

Yet he found me, I beheld him
Bleeding on the cursed tree,
Heard Him pray "Forgive them Father,
And my wistful heart said faintly

Some of Self and Some of Thee.

Day by day His tender Mercy
Healing, helping, full and free
Sweet, strong, and oh so patient
Brought me lower, while I whispered
Less of self and MORE of Thee.

Higher than the highest heavens
Deeper than the deepest sea,
Lord Thy love at last hath conquered
Grant me now my soul's desire,
None of self and ALL of Thee.

He whom thou servest, slights not even His weak ones,
No deed, though poor shall be forgot, however, feeble done.
The prayer, the wish, the thought, the faintly spoken word,
The place that seems to come to naught, each has its own reward.

The meekest angel of God, the Angel of Patience,
He walks with thee that angel kind, and gently whispers be resigned.
Bear up, bear on, the end shall tell,
The dear Lord ordereth all things well.

Then under Thursday 11th February, 1904, we read:

Spoke to M. . ... C. . .. . . about her soul and the next day she gave
her heart to Jesus. This was the first soul I was privileged to lead

to the Light. What joy it gives me. Oh Lord Jesus help me to have more of this joy.

I went to Christian Endeavour Convention. The meeting closed with a consecration service at which I again renewed my promise to Jesus.

Membership Card

VICTORIA FREE CHURCH.
Band of Hope.
This is to certify that Maggie Smith is a member of the above society having signed the following pledge:
I promise by Divine Assistance to abstain from all intoxicating liquors as beverages, and to discountenance all the causes and practices of Intemperance.
(Signed) 7th March, 1893, No. 82
JAMES. C. BARR.
Secretary.
In regard to the Bible Class of which Peggy was a member the following entry appears "I find it most interesting."

School holidays were usually spent at one of the beautiful and bracing resorts on the Firth of Clyde, or further afield in the Highlands of Scotland, and the home-life was a very happy and beautiful one indeed.

In a beautiful spiritual atmosphere, shedding abroad, in an enthusiastic girlish way the love of Jesus and unconsciously drinking in the beauty of Scottish scenery, Peggy grew from childhood to girlhood, whilst our lives, unknown to us both, were converging according to a Heavenly pre-arranged plan and in His time, we met when we were in our teens.

As I walked merrily and confidently along the Lochar Moss road en route to Glasgow on a spring morning when the earth was filled with the glory of the Lord, the unseen Angel of the Lord was guiding me unerringly towards Maxwell Park where I was handed over to "My Angel" in the flesh, a beautiful, sweet, Scotch lassie, my Peggy.

From the moment Peggy asked me my name – she was 15 and I was 17, I knew my darling possessed me, and I was hers, loving her with all my heart and soul. The flame of refining, purifying, ennobling love sweeping over my soul and from that moment I was a new being, living on a higher plane of life, although I knew not the Lord.

GOD IS LOVE.

Chapter 6
Promotions

Time doth smoothly quickly glide when there's love.
John Hugh McNaughton *Love at Home*
Unknown Hymnal

*L*ove of work, love for my sweet Peggy, and love of Glasgow, softened the long arduous hours of duty and the speeding trains passed no more quickly or smoothly than the fleeting pleasant hours, the greater portion of each day being spent on Maxwell Park Station platform.

I was in love, Heaven above was softer blue,
Earth beneath was sweeter green, and
Every duty, however, menial or tiring, was a pleasure.

After a few months, my salary was increased to 12/- per week and never was 2/- more welcome, although I was perfectly satisfied with my straightened financial position. At the end of another 12 months my wage was advanced to 14/- per week and I began to feel that life was becoming more tolerable from a material point of view. I was contentedly happy in my hard straightened circumstances, and envied no one – rich or poor.

But the event of my Railway career which brought me more sheer happiness and a real kick was just round the corner, when on the transfer of the Foreman I was quite unexpectedly promoted to the vacancy at a wage of 18/- per week.

I was delirious with joy and dispensing with the corduroys I donned my new blue cloth, silver trimmed uniform, with cap to match, with justifiable pride.

In later life I received promotions with increases in salary amounting to from £100 to £250 per annum, but the thrill that accompanied my promotion from Clerk and Porter to Foreman never came again my way with equal pleasure, or such sheer joy.

Taking charge of the station during one shift each day I supervised the carrying out of the station work generally giving more attention to the trains and the booking office, for which I was responsible, and the general working of the station.

Life had been hard, both physically and in a financial sense but filled with joy, and although it was far from easy in my new elevated position, the change for the better was very appreciable.

Financially my position was now sound, but I continued to live frugally, walking long distances to avoid expenditure on tram fares and continued to find much pleasure in free institutions such as art galleries, museums, historical places and in the parks.

On one occasion when instructed to relieve a Station Master (I would be about 19 years of age) at a large suburban station, I was very thrilled notwithstanding that I had greatest difficult in getting the staff to take me seriously on account of my youthfulness, boyish appearance, and smallness, but they did recognise that I knew my job.

During 1901, the year in which Queen Victoria died (1837-1901) I was promoted from the uniformed to clerical grade at a salary of 20/- per week, and selected to fill the much coveted position of Booking Clerk (coaching clerk in South Africa) in the Scottish International Exhibition, which was held in the beautiful Kelvingrove Park, with Glasgow University standing majestically in the background, and I greatly enjoyed my new sphere of action.

I considered my financial position was now assured and with continued frugality, my newly opened Post Office Savings account began to mount steadily until I received my South African appointment, by which time £12.0.0. was standing to my credit.

I loved the "all time" clerical work, the constant contact with passengers from all parts of the world, and the excitement of the Exhibition, but the day when my Darling Peggy spoke to me at the Booking Office door still stands out in my memory – after nearly 50 years. Sweet, beautiful, girlish, and dressed becomingly, I became, if possible, more in love with her than ever before.

Having commenced the study of shorthand in my spare moments at the Booking window, I was surprised to hear the Superintendent of Staff, the gent who said I was "awfu' sma'" remark one day to someone "He's studying shorthand" having caught me busy making outlines // ((__ , evidently making a mental note of my assiduousness at the close of the Exhibition I was transferred to the District Headquarters in a Relief capacity. The incident set the whole course of my future railway career as arriving in South Africa with "operating experiences" I was ever after looked upon as an efficient and widely experienced operating officer with a sound foundation.

From 1899 until May 1902 the Boer War raged with great fierceness and much unnecessary ruthlessness, the stubborn heroic defence of Ladysmith, Kimberley and Mafeking, the battles of Spion Kop, Tuegela, where the only son of Field Marshall Lord Roberts was killed, Stormberg, etc., etc., engaged public attention. The public re-acted emotionally and even hysterically and on the occasion of the severe reverse suffered by the Highlanders at Magersfontein, near Kimberley, public war enthusiasm reached a very low level.

As and when the sieges of the three beleaguered towns Ladysmith, Mafeking, and Kimberly, were lifted hilarious mass-hysteria filled crowds thronged the streets, squares, and parks of every town in Britain, the word "Mafficking" having been derived from the hilarious rowdy scenes witnessed when Mafeking was relieved by Plumers' forces.

On this occasion I saw an old white-haired gent roughly man-handled in St. George's Square, Glasgow, because he had the courage to be pro-Boer. He was a brave man indeed, although I consider him very foolish, to fearlessly air his opinions when surrounded by such an imperialistic crowd of city dwellers, suffering from mass hysteria.

Soldiers in bright red jackets and blue trousers, or kilts, were in evidence everywhere and army drafts were continually on the move, the ultimate destination being South Africa, twenty-two thousand of whom did not return, a great number of the casualties being due to disease brought about by military ignorance. Thousands were killed needlessly due to the blundering tactics of "old school" military officers who could not adapt themselves to warfare under South African conditions, as forced upon them by the Boers. Too proud to emulate the "Boers" men fell in thousands before the enemy whom they despised, in a military sense.

It was tragic, the sacrifice of thousands of British lives, the destroying of the Republics by overwhelming number of soldiers, horses, and equipment, the burning of houses, devastation of family life and the toll of human suffering for what – that the Jews with the aid of a few British Capitalists might gain control of the Transvaal with its gold mines.

Chamberlain and Co. had nothing to be proud of, Briton's might was defied and beaten and but for unlimited reinforcement from all over the Empire we would have had to trek from the Republics and in all probability, Britain would have had to cede the Cape Province.

But the plans of God cannot be thwarted by man's transgressions, and from the ruins of the Boer War there is arising steadily but surely, a new united South Africa with one people, two languages, one flag, and one God, even the Lord.

War was in the air, the martial spirit filled our young breasts and when I failed to gain admittance to the Royal Field Horse Artillery, I determined to reach South Africa through the medium of the Railway Service.

I was sent to many station in different parts of the country in a relief capacity, and I remember relieving Blantyre, where David Livingstone was born, Ardrossan, a small seaport town serving Ireland, Saltcoats, where I was on the day Wm. Ewart Gladstone died, and many other stations in the west of Scotland, including underground stations. The contrast between the latter and the Roucan were extreme, but my love for the railway and the joy I found in work were overflowing, flooding everything else out of my life, the thought that the life of a railwayman was the perfect one being uppermost in my mind.

Using my annual pass I visited Manchester, where the siege of Mafeking was being staged in the Bellvue Gardens by means of a beautiful pyrotechnic display on a lavish scale.

Liverpool, wet and dirty, but nevertheless interesting with its underground railways and busy streets, greatly interested me; and in Bolton, Lancashire, it was found our dialects were so different that we could not carry on a conversation – this in the heart of Britain, where English is the spoken language.

London was thoroughly enjoyable without language difficulties and with helpful, polite policemen. I visited the Tower where I saw the "Beef Eaters" and Crown Jewels, Kew Gardens, quiet, beautiful, and restful in the midst of the then world's largest City, St. Paul's Cathedral, where Holman Hunt's famous picture "The Light of the World" is seen. Westminster Abbey, with its long historical associations, Westminster Bridge, the Houses of Parliament, and the Bank of England.

Travelling on the Metropolitan Railway (underground – before electrification) was not a pleasant experience, but I enjoyed seeing the city from the tops of horse drawn busses, although they were open tops and rain beat mercilessly on the unfortunate passengers who could not find inside room.

The experiences were all wonderful to me, almost fresh from the country and with the smell of the corduroys still clinging to me.

In Scotland I visited Loch Lomond, walked along the banks of "O' bonnie Doon" made famous by the Scottish National Poet, Robert Burns. Edinburgh where I climbed to the top of Sir Walter Scott's monument, one of the most beautiful monuments in the world. Saw Holy Rood Palace, connected with much intrigue, gaiety, and Royalty. Mary Queen of Scots will forever be connected with this grand old palace which is the Headquarters of our present Royalty when they visit the capital of Scotland.

Edinburgh Castle, standing on a high rocky prominence is famous in Scottish history, and Arthur's seat a hill overlooking the town and surrounding country, was climbed, to the top, from where I got an ever-memorable view of the surrounding country.

Scotland's scenic beauty far surpasses anything I have ever seen elsewhere in its ravishing combination of green lands, winding rivers, lakes, mountains, green to the very top, woods, cattle in the meadows, sheep on the hills, and bird life, over which there hangs a deep spiritual atmosphere, a glory which proclaims the presence of God in a realistic sense. Like Jacob of old one is forced to exclaim "God is in this very place."

Old, ruined abbeys, still revealing great architectural beauty, are to be found all over the country. Built by serf labour under the lash of

Roman Catholic Priests, who lived in thatched-mud huts in degrading circumstances, whilst the church looked away indifferent to human suffering and injustice.

Crumbling castles with massive ramparts and thick walls recall the days when England was Scotland's deadly enemy and Scot fought Scot to their own undoing. The nobles leading their serfs to war neglected the lands, the fratricidal strifes leaving everyone impoverished and embittered. Many sank to rise no more whilst the luxury living priests claimed the best products of the land without any consideration for serfs and their half-starved families.

I had made rapid, sound progress in the service of the Caledonian Railway Company and was considered much above the average in proficiency and experience for my age, and my zeal knew no limits, my love for the railway overshadowing all else. But I was longing for something – probably adventure in a foreign land, and when I received a reply to a letter that I had addressed to the General Manager of the Natal Government Railways, stating that I would receive an appointment on presenting myself in Durban, I was quite excited. Someone, however, advised me to try the Cape Government Railways where there were supposed to be better prospects of receiving a better offer and I accordingly did so.

God was unerringly guiding me to South Africa and to East London especially, where it was appointed that I should meet the Lord, whilst my Angel Peggy was protecting, ennobling and purifying me with her sweet unspoken love, and the first door towards my becoming System Manager of Railways, in the mandated Territory of South West Africa, was about to swing wide open, through which I fearlessly entered to fullness of physical and spiritual life in South Africa.

Chapter 7
Farewell to Scotland

(1902)

Caledonia stern and wild,
Weet nurse for a poetic child,
Land of brown heath and shaggy wood,
Land of the mountain and the flood,
Sir Walter Scott, O Caledonia! Stern and wild

Trembling with excitement, as I did on the morning when the one-armed postman delivered the letter from the Caledonian Railway Company to Roucan Cottage, I opened the letter replying to the letter I had addressed to the Agent General for the Cape of Good Hope South Africa, Trafalgar Square, London, making enquiries re an appointment with the Cape Government Railways. Joy, oh joy, could it be true! It was scarcely believable, I was not given an appointment, but I was actually engaged in a clerical position at a commencing salary of £132 per annum, and without consideration as to the relation of the salary to living costs in South Africa, I looked upon myself as a most fortunate person. I had been offered railway work in South Africa and all else was of no account.

The letter also contained instructions to call at the Agent General's office in the following week where I would be handed my ship's passage to travel by the U.C.S.S. "German" to Cape Town.

There was not time to be lost and consequently after receiving an immediate release from "C.R." I proceeded to the Roucan where I spent the weekend, a stranger in my own home.

My parents received the news of my impending departure with mixed feelings — Africa being so far, far away where missionaries from Scotland tried to lead the heathen to Jesus, but I made the great decision and they recognised they were powerless in the matter especially as I had severed my connection with the Caledonian Railway. At Church on Sunday, where I was a complete stranger to the minister and congregation, no one was interested in my going away, parochial matters engaging their whole attention.

Returning to Glasgow accompanied by mother, I spent my last evening in Scotland in the beautiful, heavenly atmosphere in the home of the Smith family, and never had my darling looked so perfectly lovely, never had the laughter, conversation and song been so sweet and helpful, and whilst I longed fervently to tell Peggy of my love for her, with scotch cautiousness I restrained myself – the time was not yet. The Cape of Good Hope was very far away especially in those days, my future was all uncertain and my worldly possession consisted of a limited wardrobe and £12.0.0 to see me through a journey of nearly 6,000 miles, necessitating about 25 days travelling.

But I did not falter or borrow money to see me through financially.

My Angel gave me her photo, which is still one of my treasured possessions, and a wall text, which I always prominently displayed in my bachelor rooms, and it is still carefully treasured in a well-preserved condition. It reads:

> The Lord bless Thee and keep Thee,
> The Lord make his face to shine upon Thee,
> And be gracious unto Thee,
> The Lord lift up his countenance upon Thee,
> And give Thee peace
> Deut. VI. 24-26
> A farewell wish.
> M.G. Smith,
> Thurs., 21 August 1902

My Darling, the Smith family, and my uncle and aunt, together with my cousins were the only people outside railway circles to whom I bade farewell in Glasgow, having in the five happy strenuous years lived without companionship, other than with fellow railwaymen on duty. When off duty,

I found pleasure in reading, studying shorthand and in visiting the many places of interest in and around Glasgow, exhibiting the same reclusiveness as I had done when at school, and the tendency not to cultivate friendships has persistently clung to me all through my life. I could not have been otherwise, being just what I am, with no conversational ability, a desire to be alone, in addition to being a non-smoker, a total abstainer and loathing filthy talk. Nevertheless I have thoroughly enjoyed life, loving the beautiful and cultivating through reading and thinking the habit of living on a high plane of life.

If I made no friends, neither had I any enemies, and as the train drew out of the Glasgow Central Caledonian Railway Station where I stood bewildered and lonely five years previously, I was happy in the knowledge that I had been a success as a railwayman, fearless in my conduct in the sight of my fellow-men, and that I was pure, although the fiery furnace of temptation had never been far from me. To God be the Glory.

A few of my fellow railwaymen came to the station to wish me God speed on my journey, and as they sang the old Jacobite song, which was heard almost every night on the same platform, I felt calmly confident the step I was taking was the right one:

> Will ye no come back again,
> Will ye no come back again
> Better load ye cana' be,
> Will ye no come back again.

Peggy was uppermost in my thoughts as I snuggled into the corner of a third class compartment, incidentally the last time I ever travelled 3rd class, or in a night train without sleeping accommodation, and in the darkness of night we rushed through Lockereby, 8 miles from the Roucan, Ecclefechon (Eagles fighting), where Carlyle was born, Gretna Green of runaway marriages fame, and stopping at Carlisle I realised we were on English soil, Scotland having been left forever. I was en route to South Africa where I would hear for the first time that God so loved the world that he gave His only begotten son that whosoever believeth in Him should not perish but have everlasting life. Herein is love not that we loved Him, but that He loved us and gave Himself for us.

Delivering my trunk at Tilbury Docks, I made my way by handsome cab to Trafalgar Square, where I became one of a considerable company of young men en route to South Africa, from practically every Railway in Britain and Ireland for service with the C.G.R., I.M.R. (afterwards the C.S.A.R.) and R.R., as well as for the Civil Services, Police, and other Government appointments in the various provinces.

We were all young, I being one of the youngest, excited, and optimistic, and all were determined that by zealous application to duty, and integrity whilst drawing upon our "home" experience and training to give a good account of ourselves. On arrival in Cape Town were dispersed all over the sub-continent, and of all those who joined the C.G.R. Service, I rose to the highest position. All the youths with whom I was able to keep contact rose to Senior positions, although a few of the bright happy lad I met in London and on-board ship fell by the wayside.

I boarded the S.S. German of the U.C.S.S. Coy at Tillbury Docks, London, amidst the usual excitement and bustle, my wonderment being inexpressible. The 2nd Class Cabin was the some of comfort, the large dining room was much larger than the whole of the Butt en Ben at the Roucan, and of the ship itself (about 7,000 tons) exceeded my wildest dreams. My adoration, for such it was, could not be expressed.

Sailing towards the Estuary of the Thames was an unforgettable experience, as the ship sailed smoothly down the broad waters of the historic River, with Greenwich, Sandhurst, Numerous hamlets, and strange new sights on the banks.

The Thames literally swarmed with craft of all descriptions, large and small and everywhere there was an air of national importance.

The following afternoon was the scene of much hustle and bustle. Southampton Harbour where the ship filled to capacity with passengers aglow with excitement, most of whom were sailing for Africa for the first time.

After the ship weighed anchor, I stood at the rail and watched the shores of England, which was almost foreign country to me, disappearing in the "shades of night", and soon I was sleeping soundly after a sleepless night in the train and a day of active excitement in London.

The great ship was a constant source of wonder to me, I enjoyed voyaging through the Bay of Biscay, where the Drummond Castle had been wrecked a few years previously with great loss of life, and I went ashore at Funchall, where I was unfavourable impressed with the squalor and dirt of the people and place with its narrow streets.

Flying fish, porpoises and sharks were all new to me and the disappearance in the northern horizon of "the plough" (also called the Great Bear) and the gradual rising of the Southern Cross from the far southern horizon all intrigued me as the prow of the ship cleft the phosphorescent waves of the South Atlantic Ocean.

The S.S. German arrived at Cape Town on the 15th of September, 1902, having sailed from Southampton on the 22nd of August and from its spacious deck (that is, to me) I viewed:

> The fairest Cape we saw in the whole circumference
> of the world.
> Sir Francis Drake. 15 June 1580.

I viewed Table Mountain with its Table Cloth with deep, wondering, admiration, never before having seen anything to equal, in size or stateliness, and shimmering Table Bay, filled with transport of all descriptions waiting to embark the war-weary, victorious happy returning soldiers, was very impressive.

Like Lady Ann Barnaard, I walked to town being unwilling to draw upon my remaining altogether too few shillings and gazed with wonder on the mixed crowd of people in the streets – white and black, British, Dutch, German, Moslem, Malays, Bantu and Coloured, all the white people appearing to me to be prosperous and everyone appeared to be very happy in the scorching sun – for it was a very hot day.

There was a general air of freedom, of enjoyment of life and of prosperity such as I had never seen, or experienced, anywhere in Great Britain.

When reporting to the Cape Town office of the C.G.R. we were met with the exclamation "Here's another crowd of them – what are we going to do with them all", and after filling in a number of Forms I was handed a 1st Class single pass for East London, along with two or three others, the great majority being directed elsewhere. How wonderfully God was leading me – having booked a second class passage, through the Agent General, although I could not very well afford the extra money required to do so, my destination was East London as only the 2nd class passengers were sent to the Eastern System where I spent many happy years and met the Lord. His guidance never faileth, and in His goodness he opened a door through which I entered to become "Trains Clerk" (senior operating officer) I Eat London in record time, and thus early gained a firm footing on the first rung of the ladder leading to System Managership.

Leaving Cape Town on the night of the 15th of September, 1902, I experienced the slowest, coldest, most foodless, and least comfortable journey every. The train was lit by means of a travelling electric dynamo as far as Touws River, from where inferior oil lamps were the sole means of lighting, and I lay shivering on the top bunk of a new C.G.R. saloon (now used for native passengers) minus a bed as I could not spare 3/- from my almost exhausted funds. All honour to the £12.0.0 with which I left Glasgow, and which had seen me through the long journey notwithstanding the constant drain on such a slender sum.

Extras could not be thought of, and food had to be kept down to two meals (poor ones at that) per day, but I was joyously happy, with no thought of hardship, or shortage of funds, and journeys end was in sight.

It is interesting to recall that many years subsequently I travelled over the same rail route, in my own luxurious private saloon, with dining compartment, lounge, two bed compartments, bath, with hot and cold water – conveniences, attendant's room, pantry, and a fully equipped kitchen. The goodness of the Lord faileth never.

Trains laden with soldiers, singing and making merry, were crossed at almost every station and siding in the Karroo, which I connected with Robert Moffatt and David Livingstone, Peggy having presented me with a copy of the Life of Robert Moffatt sometime before I left Scotland. It is still on our bookshelf.

De Aar, where the City of London (C.I.V.) volunteers received a warm if hostile reception, from the Boers before detraining, and which station fell under my control when I was Superintendent at Kimberley, Neaauwpoort connected with Major Haig (Field Marshall Earl Haig of World War No. I) and Stormberg, the scene of General Gatacre's serious reverse, were all familiar names to me and of great interest. Bushman's Hoek, where any preconceived ideas I may have entertained in regard to Railways were shattered, the thought that a Railway could be constructed sheer up the face of such a mountain, or that engines could haul trains over such steep grades never having occurred to me in semi-flat Britain.

The Natives were a source of wonderment, dressed in old, ragged garments, soldiers' tunics, and any oddment irrespective of the sex for which it was originally intended. Laughing, dancing, shouting to each other in a strange language with loud pitched voice and forever asking with cupped hands "a pennie baas", "'n stukkie brood" or "Sonke, bass".

Excitement prevailed on the third morning as we dropped down, and down from Blaney Junction towards sea level at East London, and the tang of the sea air from the Indian Ocean entered our nostrils. We were delirious with joy of youth, without a care, in the world and happy in the knowledge that our great adventure was reaching the climax for which the voyage had been undertaken, e.g., to commence work on the C.G.R. The future was before me, I had health and strength on my side with a sound knowledge of railway work to see me through on the practical side of life. But a life of wider scope and true joy such as I knew not yet, was just ahead of me.

I walked along Oxford Street in the early hours of the morning, saw the Buffalo River, and the beautiful beach which was undeveloped with no houses nearer than the Quigney. Ox wagons, loaded with vegetables and produce, filled the large market square and early risers were arriving by foot and bicycle to purchase the household vegetables in one of the best markets in the world.

The peaceful scene was far removed from the clanging noise of city life as I had experienced it in Glasgow, in a perfectly beautiful setting.

At Railway Headquarters for the Eastern System I was informed that I was being posted to Sterkstroom, as coaching Clerk, and spending my 4th night in the train again without a bed, I arrived at my destination breakfastless but happy and ready to meet the requirements of my new position, with about 2/- in my possession.

When I approached the Agent General in London for an appointment, £12. 0. 0. stood to my credit in the Post Office Saving Bank, with which I had to augment my slender wardrobe, travel through London, give tips to stewards on board ship (one steward was very nasty when I handed him the sum of 10/`) spend a day in Cape Town and 3 days and 4 nights in the train. The Lord sustained me, and I was able to thoroughly enjoy everything from start to finish, except when shivering in the cold travelling over the Hex River Pass, without worrying about how I was going to get through, but I never spent a penny which could be saved for future absolute necessities.

My passage money (£24) had been advanced by the Government which I repaid at the rate of £2.0.0. monthly out of my commencing salary of £11.0.0 per month.

> Go work today in my vineyard.
> St. Matt. 21:28
>
> Go work in my vineyard, sweet is the joy of toil,
> Sow freely in abundance great and water well the soil,
> Time will deck the harvest field, with precious ripened grain,
> God's husbandry is in precious souls, His blessing is your gain.
>
> Go work in my vineyard, tell men of Christ, today
> Without the Light in darkness, far straying off the way
> Now is the time accepted, loved ones lost, to gain
> In my vineyard beautiful, sin left its ugly stain.
>
> Go work in my vineyard, hear the Master's call
> The day's far spent and weary ones, by the wayside fall,
> Give yourself in kindly deeds, and friendly help today,
> Straying ones in gladness bring, to Christ the living Way
> J.R.
> Johannesburg. 6 September 1946.

Chapter 8
Sterkstroom

(1902)

*T*he station Master, Sterkstroom, an Aberdonian Scot, kindly, sympathetic and withal a good disciplinarian, received me in an encouraging manner, and after satisfying himself in regard to my experience on the Caledonian Railways from which Railway company he also hailed, he took me to the Booking Office and left me to make the best of my new job, with the remark "You'll manage, all right!!" I did, but in the strange circumstances it was a hard struggle.

There was no turning back, but what with my complete lack of even an elementary knowledges of the "Taal", or an acquaintance with a few needful native words, or phrases, and quite at a loss in regard to the Railway geography of the country including the Rhodesias, there were many times when I was at a loss what to do, but I had the will to overcome difficulties and I did — somehow.

Natives, travelling to and from the Transkei, passed through Sterkstroom in great numbers, Indwe being at that time their entraining and detraining stations, and I was much distressed, leave alone horrified at the barefaced manner in which they were robbed of small change by railwaymen and in overcharging, one man (a clerk) made as much as £5 .0 .0 per day, and several others were not far behind. One of these barefacedly informed me what was being done, and how, and unashamedly asked me to fall into line, but I firmly refused and incurred their displeasure. They were afraid that my honesty would reveal their dishonesty, and it would but for slackness in the Audit Department.

The Natives were crowded into "native trucks" – really cattle trucks without drinking water or sanitary conveniences, attached to goods trains, and in every respect, they were treated similarly to the slaughter cattle en route to Johannesburg abattoirs. As a matter of fact, if anything, the cattle were treated with more consideration and less harshness.

At Sterkstroom I saw a huge swarm of locusts, such as I only saw once again many years afterwards, in South West Africa, when trains stood helpless on the slippery rail, made so by squashed locusts, everything was devoured in the precious vegetable gardens and on the veld, and the veld was left a barren wilderness of sand. My previous knowledge of locusts was that John the Baptist according to the Bible, ate locusts and wild honey. Incidentally, there is a tribe of natives near Hamaskraal, Transvaal, who grind dried locusts into a meal and eat them so prepared, and I saw a large number of natives near Louis Trichard eating handfuls of live flying ants.

During my stay at Sterkstroom I visited Indwe where the S. A. coal used in C. G. R. engines was mined. Stoney, hard, unburnable stuff with low calorific value and when unmixed with imported Welsh coal, two firemen were required to maintain the needful pressure of steam in the engine boiler. Meno who actually fired engines under these conditions told me it was murderous work.

I resided with a Dutch family, who could speak but little English, and I knew no "taal" whatever. They were a homely, cleanly, friendly quiet family, who did not appear to have been over embittered by the war, and I was not only comfortable but happy in their home, the only drawback being the scarcity of water due to the prevailing drought.

Life on the whole was gloriously pleasant, how could it be otherwise in the bright sunshine, after Glasgow's fog, rain, snow and underground railway, with the wide open veld stretching away and away to the far horizon for every calling me to roam over its illimitable space, Penhoek in the Stormberg range touching the blue sky and the friendliness of everyone, Boer or Briton, although I did not make permanent friends. How could I, a young man who indulged in none of the friendly matters and I was not interested in church.

The train loads of evacuees returning from the concentration camp at East London to their devastated farms and homes in the Orange Free State and Transvaal, were a sight, sorrowful, depressing and humiliating to me. There was no laughter, or not of joy amongst the poor broken, dismayed, and forlorn women and children who sat looking out of the carriage windows with eyes that did not see, and with ears that did not hear. They were returning as they thought, to a future of despair, when under the hated Union Jack they would have to toil for their Imperial Over Lords, but as the dawning of a new area broken in upon their despairing outlook, they resolutely set themselves to repair the waste, to restore the ravages of war and under responsible Government granted by a trusting generous Liberal Government in Britain, not only did they manage to re-establish themselves, but they also gained government control.

> To know the love of Christ which passeth knowledge.
> Eph. 3:19.

> Till we all come in the Unity of the Faith and of the knowledge of the Son of God, unto a perfect man, unto the measure and the stature of the fulness of Christ.

> Eph. 4:13

> A friend loveth at all times.
> Prov: 17.17.

Mr J. Rogan

East London, 1904. Aged 23.

(Right) East London, 1906. Aged 25

Chapter 9
East London – Burghersdorp – Molteno

(1902-1904)

For the second time, I approached East London by train in the early morning a few days before Christmas, 1902, having been transferred to the Operating Section in the office of the Assistant Traffic Manager, as a direct outcome of the Caledonian Superintendent having seen me practising shorthand in the Caledonian Railway Exhibition Booking Office.

I kept up my studies of this useful commercial acquisition and in 1904 I took second place in the C.G.R. shorthand annual contents held in Cape Town which was open to all railwaymen. For this achievement I was awarded an increase of £10 per annum, thus gaining seniority over my £11.0.0 per month compatriots, which advantage I never lost throughout the long years that lay ahead.

Making myself thoroughly proficient in the Regulations pertaining to the Single Line Trains Control, and all other aspects of operating work I was looked upon as a valuable experienced operating officer, with considerable typing ability. I loved the work, and East London, without making fast friends, or attending a church, but the Lord was gradually and surely leading me towardss the greatest awakening of my life – my conversion.

The year 1903 was an uneventful one in so far as my railway life was concerned, beyond that my salary was increased from £130 to £144.0.0. per annum, and I had still to practice rigid economy as I had done in Glasgow, but not to the same extent. This was no hardship, however, and I considered myself to be well off on the whole, and I was very happy.

During this year I suffered considerably from recurring attacks of Hay fever, which I now consider was nothing else than a mild form of malaria, of which disease the railway doctor had no knowledge, and towards the end of the year I was ordered away from the coast for health reasons.

Burghersdorp in Karroo, sun-drenched, unbearably hot, in the dread grip of a long severe drought, with war's deadening aftermath hanging over the whole district, was my next venue, where the Dutch were sullen and resentful towards the small English-speaking community, and on the whole non-co-operative.

I lived in bachelor quarters and dined in the hotel where £6.0.0. per month was charged for food only. It was barefaced robbery, but I had no option in the matter and the hotel proprietor knew he had me as well as the others in his grip.

When at Burghersdorp the drought broke and a rain deluged the countryside for days. What have been a burning stretch of sand became a raging-wide-torrent, carrying everything before it, and crossing a deep wide spruit in darkness I missed my foot on the narrow plank, and fell into deep strongly running water, being nearly drowned.

Life was not exciting, and, on the whole, I preferred Sterkstroom, therefore, when after a few months only, I received notice of a transfer to Molteno, I was not at all sorry.

Snow lay deep in Stormberg when I arrived at Molteno, and I shivered in biting cold, in bright sunshine, much as I had never experienced in Scotland. It was cold.

The work, of which there was not very much, was much too easy for a young energetic man, and I spent many hours roaming over the veld, reading, idling, and generally uselessly passing the time until sometime early in 1904 when, to my delight, I was re-transferred to East London.

I loved the up-country life – South Africa had gripped me in its warm, peaceful, loving embrace and Scotland had disappeared altogether out of my existence.

That ye might be filled with all the fulness of God
Eph. 3:19.

Lord fill my heart with love Divine,
Keep pure my thoughts, noble and sublime,
Teach me, Lord, Thy face to seek,
To walk with Thee in spirit meek.
J.R.
Johannesburg. 30 November 1946.

Chapter 10
East London

(1904-1910)

For the third time, I approached East London travelling by train in the early morning, the sun was rising dressed in golden hues, over the calm Indian Ocean and the peaceful little town was awaking to another day.

Early bathers were wending their way to the Beach, marketers walking and riding on horseback were en route to the large up to date market hall, and natives, laughing, shouting, and gesticulating, wended their way from the location on the side of the hill towards the town, to commence another day's work in town. The scene and surroundings were all dear to me, my beloved East London, and my good fortune in getting retransferred to East London seemed too good to be true. But the Lord was leading me step by step to the trysting place where He would be me face to face at the foot of the cross, and lead me into newness and fullness of life.

The severe depression of 1904-1910, the aftermath of the Boer War, which cast its devastating evil effects over the whole of South Africa, was beginning to rear its ugly head an in the Operating section of the Railways, the volume of work, compared with the time when I was there previously, had greatly diminished, and severe retrenchments together with drastic Government financial restrictions were under way. Salaries were subjected to a temporary reduction of 5%, every male had to pay Income Tax on an income of over £50 per annum. Young, experienced railwaymen, most of whom had resigned from service with oversea Railway Companies to take up a position with the C.G.R. were retrenched in great numbers, and many were thus ruined in their prospects of a career for life.

Married railwaymen could not maintain their homes, many houses stood unoccupied, whilst lovely houses were disposed of for less than the bond on them. Fires deliberately started were so numerous that the Insurance Companies insisted on an efficient fire brigade being brought into being, a relief camp for workless men was opened at Chiselhurst, and many workless – hungry, walked to Johannesburg and elsewhere where the labour market was no better.

My enthusiasm and zealousness for the railway never flagged, through all the depressing years my confidence that somehow or other better days were ahead, and my Heavenly Father kept me under His protecting wing until prosperity returned to the land. At the time retrenchment was rampant, it appeared to me that I would have to be one of the unfortunate ones but the Lord, intervening on my behalf, put into the heart of the Traffic Manager to reshuffle his administrative staff to make room for me, whom he scarcely knew — thus clearly indicating the Lord's guiding hand in the matter.

I continued to assiduously practice shorthand, with a view to increasing my speed (and I did), I also studied the "Cape Taal" with some success and in the Operating office I was practically the only clerk who could fill my position in the section in addition to being a qualified station clerk.

My ability to write shorthand at speed was taken advantage of by the Management and I was required to attend Accident and other Enquiries to take a verbatim note of the proceedings. This necessitated a fair amount of travelling, and consequently I became thoroughly acquainted not only with the outside staffs, but also with the lay-out of the stations and the physical features of the Line generally.

The Management of the "East London Daily Dispatch" asked me on occasions to undertake special fast reporting and amongst others I reported verbatim political speeches made by Dr. Jameson, of "The Raid" fame, Dr. Smart, at one time Minister of Railways and Sir Gordon Sprigg whose political career extended back many years, and at one time he was contemporary with Cecil John Rhodes.

Feeling ran very high at these political meetings, many references being made to Mugwumps "The Bond", of which much is written in the Life of Cecil John Rhodes and in Cape History, and other flag-waving references.

I travelled, in turns, with other members of the staff on the monthly Pay Train, all over the system, paying the staff and distributing stores. A slow, expensive, cumbersome arrangement the necessity for which existed only in the minds of the old Cape regime. To us youngsters it was a glorious 13-day picnic, living in a caboose, stabling during night wherever we happened to be, and dawdling along with line without thought to time.

Due to the depression we all had very little to do, passenger traffic and tonnage being at their lowest, with empty passenger trains, although the passenger train services were very much restricted with no development work whatever.

Unfortunately increases in salary were not granted on our minus 5% small salaries, promotion was at a standstill and no one outside high financial circles could foresee how long the black cloud of depression was going to hang over the land. The Government, who had found Millions of pounds to assist Britain's war effort, callously brought about circumstances which created unemployment, caused much suffering and drove many fine young men including South African born lads out of the country.

The future did not worry me, my faith in my ultimate progress in the railway service being unimpaired or dimmed, and optimistically during 1908 I suggested to my Angel Peggy that we should become engaged, at which time she was in the Mission Field in India, and to my great joy my offer was accepted.

My bachelorhood years which I always connect with East London, drew to a close smoothly, and happily — I should almost say joyously, and during March, 1910, I joined the R.M.S. Kenilworth Castle at Cape Town en route to Scotland to meet my Angel having arranged to be married in Peggy's home church – Titwood Parish Church.

My salary was £168 per annum, and I was in about the third senior position in operating office, or a third-grade clerk in the railway grading system.

Chapter 11
My Conversion

I consider the greatest and most far-reaching event in my life for all time was the act of surrendering my life, body, soul, and spirit, to the Lord Jesus Christ, in East London Town Hall, during the year 1904.

Meeting "My Angel" at Maxwell Park, Glasgow, entering the service of the Caledonian Railways, my emigration to South Africa, our engagement and subsequent marriage, were all strikingly important events, but the meet the Lord in "The Way" – His Way – and to be born again into newness of life controlled by God, was an experience which will forever eclipse all else in my life.

"I being in the Way" the Lord found me and in full and glad surrender I yielded my self-centred worldly self – my all – to Him who has promised never to leave me, nor forsake me, and in the 45 years I have known him He never has.

Shy, retiring, avoiding company, as much as possible, friendly, without making friends, spending my leisure studying, I grew listless and vaguely dissatisfied with myself, and everything in general, except my beloved railway, but continued to retain my inward happiness. It was clearly the work of the Holy Spirit driving me away from my complacent self, into a state of heart and mind, and a place where the Saviour could meet me, at His trysting place, the foot of the Cross. The daily, constant, prayer, of my Beloved Peggy, who had prayed for me continuously since our first meeting during 1898 was heard at the throne of grace, and on aimlessly entering the Baptist church, East London, after an ill-spent Sunday, I was convicted of my sinful condition during the singing of the hymn: --

> There is a fountain filled with blood,
> Drawn from Immanuel's veins,
> And sinners plunged beneath that flood,
> Loose all their guilty stains.
> Hymn No. 174
> The Church Hymnary (1902)

I was convicted but not converted, and the next few days, with the words of the beautiful appealing hymn set to an arresting tune constantly rhyming in my ears, were miserable indeed, and without knowing the reason, I felt something had to happen.

The Holy Spirit was striving with me mightily, and in this mood, I was Divinely led to attend an Evangelistic meeting conducted by the fine Preacher, Singer, Gipsy Smith, then being used mightily by the Lord in the conversion of souls in the East London Town Hall. The Lord had performed a miracle in getting me into the meeting, and once inside, I felt immediately under the complete power of the Holy Spirit.

The large mixed choir, the joyous confident singing of Moody and Sankey Hymns, the packed, expectant, happy crowd of people and the powerful direct appeal of the preacher, who seemed to know all about me, delivered in the power of the Holy Spirit, held me as in their inescapable spell. The atmosphere of the meeting was such as I had never before experienced, not even in the "John McNeill" Evangelistic meetings in Glasgow, and as the Preacher unfolded God's wonderful plan of salvation, through the death of His Only Son, Jesus, during which he faithfully brought to light my lost and ruined condition, I saw myself the sinner for whom Christ died. Could it be true – the Preacher said it was – my own conscience confirmed what he said about me, and I knew that the moment to make the Great decision had arrived, and that there was no escape. To accept, or reject, the Christ had to be squarely faced during what might be my last opportunity.

Quietly, unostentatiously, but decidedly I surrendered my life to the Lord Jesus Christ, and I had the witness within myself that I was saved. Along with many others I entered the enquiry room a condemned soul, and knew that I had passed from death into life. Henceforth my one desire would be to know Him and the power of His resurrection.

Oh happy day that fixed my choice,
On Thee my Saviour and my God
Well may this glowing heart rejoice,
And tell its raptures all abroad.
Hymn No. 404
The Church Hymnary (1902)

Nothing in my hand I bring,
Simply to Thy Cross I cling.
Hymn No. 191
The Church Hymnary (1902)

Come what may, I had found the Christ, who had made me his willing captive, and I counted not the cost nor reckoned the road would be an easy one. One thought, and one thought only possessed me and that was the fact that I had found the Christ, who is the Son of God and as I walked out into the cool of the night:

Heaven above was softer blue,
Earth beneath was sweeter green,
Something lived in every hue,
Christless eyes had never seen,
Birds with gladder song o'erflow,
Flowers with deeper beauty shine,
Since I know as now I know
That I am His, and He is mine.
I am his and he is mine
Wade Robinson (1890)

The constant pleading, faithful prayers of "My Angel" made in the faith that God hears and answers prayer had been heard, and fully answered, and I immediately wrote telling my Darling of my newfound joy and new life.

What the world would think, or say, did not concern me, I had found the Lord, who had waited patiently for me from my youth.

Be ye transformed, be renewed, wrote St. Paul in His epistle to the Romans, and Christ said "Ye must be born again", and in His resurrection power I took my place amongst my fellow railwaymen, who were always tolerant and sympathetic, where I witnessed fearlessly for my Lord.

A spending band of Y.M.C.A. young men workers, unknown to me, effectively encircled my life and it was not long before I was the Y.M.C.A. Evangelistic Secretary, addressing meetings in a very imperfect amateurish manner, haltingly leading prayer meetings, and arranging speakers and leaders for the various spiritual activities of the Y.M.C.A.

Oh, the abundant joy of the new found life, the lasting satisfaction and the joy of witnessing for Christ in the power of the Holy Spirit.

From a life of aimless drift, apart from the railway, with shyness, awkwardness and reclusiveness overcome, I became the centre of the Evangelistic work of the Y.M.C.A., in close touch with the spiritual activities of the protestant churches.

On my return to East London from a short recuperative trip to Queenstown, the following paragraph appeared in the Y.M.C.A. news of the "Daily Dispatch":

> "Mr. Rogan, is one of the mainstays of the spiritual department of our work, where his cheery smile, and quiet enthusiasm, encourages and stimulates all who come in contact with him."

The churches, St. George's Presbyterian Church included, were not too sympathetic towards the Gipsy Smith Converts, but Dr. Geo Blair, who arrived in Scotland soon as the conclusion of the Mission, infused a new spirit into St. George's with the result that there was a great soul awakening and much needed enthusiasm for the things of the Lord. But churchism was dominant and apart from the Christian Endeavour Moment it was not easy to "speak a word for Jesus".

From before 1904 until about 1908 the Christian Endeavour Moment was strong in East London and in S. A. generally, and it was not long before I was appointed President of St. George's Branch, where 30 to 50 young men and women met once a week to praise the Lord in Song, for study of the Word, and take part in chain prayer. A finer, more spiritually minded, and more enthusiastic Band of young men and women I have never met, who would have been a tremendous power in the church and community if only they had been permitted and encouraged by the minister, elders, and others.

I was a Sunday School teacher in St. George's Church and had the joy of meeting my boys in several widely separated places in the Union. One of them is (1949) in a very senior position in the Mechanical Dept. in Pretoria, and other two are at the top of the business world in Johannesburg.

Not content with being fully occupied in the Y.M.C.A., Christian Endeavour, and Sunday School, I engaged in Coloured Mission work in the Bayswater Road area (a Wesleyan work) as Sunday School Superintendent and subsequently I was asked by the Wesleyan Minister to become their General Superintendent of the work. It was an important work, but the fickleness of the poor unfortunate people was too terrible for words. They could pray pleadingly and beautifully, profess tearful contrition, sing lustily as well as sweetly the church hymns and attend church regularly until such time as there was a quarrel, which was not at all infrequent, when the life of the church and the coloured community would be disrupted for weeks on end.

Together with an enthusiastic band of the Lord's children I took part in a weekly open air meeting and preached occasionally in St. Paul's and the West Bank Presbyterian Churches, when I generally attracted good congregations, but looking back I can easily see that educationally and in spiritual growth I was not qualified, for preaching being still an infant in Christ, unable to tell the people through actual everyday experiences, what the Lord had done for me. Nevertheless, the winning of precious souls was my whole desire and constant prayer. I also preached occasionally in one of the small Wesleyan Churches.

The Annual Y.M.C.A. Camp held on the Beach in East London during the Christmas holidays was a source of fine fellowship and much inspiration to me, with a spiritual and ennobling influence, moulding my life in the formative years of my spiritual growth.

And so the happy, spirit-filled years 1904-1910 fled past quickly in work filled hours which stored my mind with pleasant memories, the terrible commercial depression and stagnation of promotion being unable to dim the joy by gloom, pessimism, or financial worry, I had found the Lord where only He can be found, at the foot of the Cross, where I knelt in lowly contrition and acknowledged Him as my Saviour and Redeemer.

Christ is not found in political organisations, church membership, social standing, in monied circles or fame, but only at the Cross. Only the Son of God, by His death and Resurrection can "make the sinner clean" and give to him life abundant.

> God so loved the world of sinners lost
> And ruined by the fall
> To know Him and the power of His Resurrection is
> The secret of victorious living in Christ who is
> The hope of Glory, The Way, The Truth, and The Life
> [unknown]

It is all so simple and wonderful, Christ died for sinner and herein is His love revealed, not that we loved Him, but the He loved us and gave Himself for us and that includes me, the vilest of sinners.

> God so loved the world that he gave His only begotten Son that whosoever believeth in Him should not perish but have everlasting life.
> John 3:16

> Therefore give not only our all to Him, which is easy, but ourselves, body, soul, and spirit.
> [unknown]

A PRAYER

Ask and it shall be given you.

Give me a thought on which to live,
And strenuous hours of work and play.
Give me the zeal my best to give,
And kindly deeds to do today.

Give me a word of cheer for all,
And love that leaps o'er creed and race.
Give me pure thoughts towards one and all,
And sympathy for self efface.

Give me a vision God of Thee,
And moments filled with love Divine,
Give me Thyself, come live in me,
And make this human temple thing.

J.R.
Windhoek,
    S.W.A.
        2 February 1941.

Margaret Gillieson Smith

Aged 22 Years   **Aged 24 Years(Taken in India)**

Chapter 12
Peggy

1904-1910

All my waking thoughts were of My Angel as I travelled Southwards on the night of the 22nd of August, 1902, and my darling in her parents' lovely home at Maxwell Park was lonely, but with the sweet assurance that her Saviour was very near to comfort and to strengthen. Our unspoken love for each other was deep and unshakeable, and we believed that God would, in His own good time, open up the way for us to be joined together in Holy Matrimony.

Peggy was advancing rapidly in her commercial career, where her skill and zealousness were acknowledged by the management and workers.

Life in the home went on much as usual, with an annual holiday generally to one of the Firth of Clyde resorts, assisting domestically in the evening and generally giving of her best in every direction.

Fully surrendered to Jesus, my Darling found great pleasure in her Sunday School and Church activities, teaching in a relief capacity, working in a slum on the South side of Glasgow together with a youthful band of Christ-filled enthusiasts and assisting in meetings. Hers was a full life, and when workers were required for the Kalimpong Inter-Denominational Eurasian Children's Homed, Kalimpong near Darjeeling, India, Peggy was selected out of a large number of applicants and sailed for that far-off land on the 18th of November, 1904.

Dr. J. A. Graham, K.I.H. Medal, First Class order, who founded the Homes, was delighted with the appointment, as Peggy's sister Lizzie, who was already in the work, had proved a great success, and the Rev. W. H.

Rankine, B.D., of Titwood Parish Church, of which Peggy was a very active member, was proud of the fact that another member of his church was added to the long roll of missionaries who had gone forth from his congregation on missionary service.

I had just recently surrendered to the Lord and was very happy indeed in the knowledge that my Darling had been led by the Lord to volunteer for missionary service in the foreign field, and that she was considered worthy of such an honour. The contract was for 5 years — hence we could not meet before early in 1910, but like Jacob of old, I was deeply in love and knew the years would "quickly — smoothly" fly.

The steamship service between India and South Africa was aggravatingly inconvenient, slow, and irregular, and not infrequently six weeks or so passed before we heard from each other, but the spirit-filled, inspiring letters, breathing deep devotion to the Lord and the work to which Peggy was consecrated meant more than anything else to me, and when received, the long wait in between disappeared in the joy and assurance they gave to me.

The voyage from Liverpool to Calcutta [Kolkata] in the "SS City of Calcutta", via Gibraltar, Malta, the Red Sea, and Columbo was a memorable one to my Darling, and the train journey to Siliguri, followed by a two-days journey on horseback were thoroughly enjoyed. Everything was so strange, with Indian people who, although predominating in numbers, were not in charge of their own country.

A good working knowledge of the language was one of the first tasks requiring to be taken in hand, and my Angel soon proved adept in acquiring a good knowledge of Hindustani.

At the commencement, Peggy was an "Aunty", e.g., second in charge of a cottage with between 20 and 30 Eurasian boys, but before long, having proved thoroughly capable, although still very young, she was promoted to "House Mother" in charge of a cottage housing 28 boys. A great responsibility for a young woman, but Peggy was equal to the demands of the task with her usual resourcefulness, and in the "power of the spirit", she managed the home in an efficient and economical manner, winning the affection of the boys and admiration of everyone else.

During 1908, although South Africa was still in the throes of a very severe commercial depression, obscuring all signs of advancement in the Railway or Government Services, I was definitely led by the Lord to ask my Darling, whom I had then known for 10 years, to agree to our becoming engaged, and to my joy she accepted my proposal. To me, it all seemed too good to be true, but the Lord was with us, and He who had hitherto helped us would not desert us in the future.

Sailing from Calcutta in the "SS City of Benares", Peggy, after a pleasant voyage via the Red Sea, spent Christmas Day, 1909, in London, from where she proceeded to Maxwell Park to prepare for our marriage early in 1910. The following is an extract from "The Missionary Record of the United Free Church, Scotland":

March, 1910

KELVINGROVE CHURCH

Last Sabbath, we had an address from Miss Maggie Smith, a worker in the Church of Scotland Homes at Kalimpong, India, and a friend of one of our Teachers. By happy coincidence, this was "India" day in our own church.

Miss Smith gave a very interesting account of her day's work with 28 boys (practically orphans) in these homes, and brought home with vivid realism the happier lot of children in Glasgow. Her appearance in the strange Indian costume left a strong impression on the children, who sat with eager attention — eyes and mouth open — from beginning to end, and we all feel that we listened to one of the very best lessons we have ever heard.

Miss Smith is a very gifted teacher, and her address had given every one of us a more living interest in Mission Work abroad in general and in India in particular.

Mr. and Mrs. J. Rogan

Glasgow — 1910

Chapter 13
Marriage

1910

As the London to Glasgow express train drew quickly and smoothly into the Dumfries Station, my Darling, a vision of sweet loveliness, was standing on the platform to greet me, and the long years of separation melted like mist before the rising sun in the joy of our meeting, never more to separate until one or the other is called to our Eternal Home. Behind and in the meeting lay glorious victory for us both, love having triumphed over 8 years of separation with the wide Indian Ocean between us.

The heavy, four-wheeled horse-drawn cab lumbered over the rough macadamised Roucan road, which I had walked so frequently in all weather, sunshine, rain, sleet, and snow, not forgetting the fierce North gales as we nestled close to each other in this long-waited-for hour and freely gave thanks to our Heavenly Father, who had so wondrously kept us in His care from that day when we met, according to His arrangement, at Maxwell Park.

Our faith in the ultimate outcome of our having been brought together in pure, holy love never faltered, and we looked forward to the fast-approaching day when we would be united in marriage in quiet, steady confidence.

The Roucan, old, fast asleep in the bosom of its ancient glory, held no attraction for us, beyond my again seeing my parents, both of whom had aged considerably, the fact that Peggy was able to make their acquaintance, so after a few days wandering around in a strange atmosphere where I had scampered so joyously in childish glee, we left for Maxwell Park, Glasgow.

Mr. & Mrs. Smith and family gave us a right hearty welcome, but, oh my — the station — could it be that this small, beautiful, suburban station, through which small engines hauling small coaches filled with what appeared to me as dull, business-occupied people, was the place where I had cleaned windows, scrubbed floors, booked passengers, and wore a corduroy uniform in a spirit of sheer joy that changed long hours and drudgery into a heaven on earth? It was probably nothing had changed, the change being in me, and I hoped the boys, now working 8-hour shifts, found the same joy and satisfaction in their work as I had found.

Of course, thy had not the inexpressible happiness as I had in waiting for and seeing the sweetest girl of all time joining and alighting from the trains and occasionally accompanying her to the garden gate.

Our wedding was arranged for the 29th of April, 1910, and I spent a few days in the Y.M.C.A., Glasgow, when I wrote the following "Remembrances" to myself:

Y.M.C.A., Room 93,
Bothwell Street,
Glasgow.
26 April 1910.

Remember

----

1. Your declaration of love to Peggy, and how, in the sight of God, you have to love and cherish her.

2. She is your wife (Ephesians 5th Chap. And 25th verse), a woman, and a child of God, born in Jesus Christ, our Saviour.

3. That love begets love, smiles beget smiles, and a happy home reflects the joy.

4. Your cheerfulness as a bachelor, in the Y.M.C.A., C.E., S.S., and other meetings, and remember such cheerfulness is now required in your home first.

5. The statement of God in the 13th Chap. Of 1st Corinthians about love never failing.

6. The better your life and the nearer to God in Christ, so shall the temptations of your children be made easier to overcome.

7. Christ in God, and <u>us</u> in Christ, heirs of Salvation, and thereby we will be called to give an account of the deeds done in the flesh.

(signed) John Rogan.

Then the following prayer:

Prayer

Lord, I pray earnestly that our whole life may be a gradual enfolding and unfolding of Thy Will. May we be in harmony with Thee — each other — and our environments. Bless us and make us a blessing at all times, and make our home a very gateway to Heaven.

At the altar in Titwood Parish Church, Pollokshields, Glasgow, the Rev. W.H. Rankine, B.D., who was Peggy's spiritual Father, joined us in holy matrimony, and congratulations were showered upon us at the large reception held in the church hall after the ceremony.

My darling looked radiantly beautiful in her silk dress and long veil, and bouquet of flowers, whilst I was dressed in a frock coat with the accompanying "Tile hat" — the only time I was ever so clad, except when I dressed for our wedding photograph.

God's Angel — my Angel Peggy, who asked me my name at Maxwell Park station platform in 1869 — was my wife, my very own, and the years of separation were forgotten in our joy of each other.

Wedding Group

Titwood Church. Pollokshields, Glasgow. 1910

L. to R. front row: Miss S.B. Smith, Mr. J. Rogan, Mrs. Rogan, Miss Edith Smith, MR. J. Bell, Miss M.I. Smith. Back row: Rev. Rankie, Mr. A.G. Smith, Mrs. A.G. Smith, Mr. J. Rogan, Sr., Rev. Mackenzie.

As the train emerged from the city of Glasgow into the beautiful green countryside of Lanarkshire, we knelt in prayer and gave Him thanks for His great goodness to us and asked that He would impart to us the grace, courage, and steadfastness to continue with Him throughout all the days of our life. Moffat, where we spent the first part of our honeymoon, is a beautiful, quiet, rural town situated among hills in the South of Scotland, and from there we travelled to the lakes of Killarney, Ireland, made world famous with the song "Killarney" in which the sweet, spiritual beauty of the lakes is faithfully portrayed, but not matched, in word and music.

When sailing down the broad River Clyde, much excitement was created by the ship's gear going out of order, causing the vessel to swing from bank to bank of the river, and it had to return to the starting basin in Glasgow before it could be faced in the direction of Ireland.

The meeting of the ocean well at the mouth of the Firth proved disastrous for our honeymoon voyage as Peggy, becoming seasick, disappeared to the Ladies Cabin, and I did not see her again until we reached the Port of Queenstown some 40 hours later.

When partaking of breakfast at Queenstown, the waiter recited to us, in a delightful, soft, Irish voice "The Bells of Shannon" and on arrival at Killarney, we immediately commenced exploring the beautiful lakes and the historical places of interest in the neighbourhood.

The sweet, spiritual beauty, the restfulness, and the charm of the lakes and surroundings cannot be captured by the pen, nor can the meanness of the houses in the town and the degradation and filth of the Roman Catholic inhabitants who live under the shadow of a magnificent Cathedral be faithfully described. In my travels, the nearest approach I have seen to the squalor and deadening spirit of Roman Catholicism experienced in Killarney was at Funchal on Madeira Island.

Whilst driving in an Irish jaunting car, the driver solemnly informed us that the Roman Catholics and Protestants were so well disposed towards each other that they went to each others' funerals, and from what I saw generally, I should imagine the Roman Catholics looked upon such functions with considerable pleasure when a Protestant filled the hearse.

On the way to the World's Christian Endeavour Convention, Liverpool, we spent a few hours in Dublin, where the sears of rebellion were plainly visible, and when crossing the Irish Channel, Kingston to Holyhead, my bride again disappeared to the Ladies Lounge, leaving me to travel alone. The voyage across the Channel was the roughest I have ever experienced, with huge waves breaking over the ship, and I believe I was the only passenger who escaped sickness. In any case, I was the only one on deck.

About 5,000 people from all parts of the world attended the Liverpool World's C. E. Convention, where the Crucified and Risen Lord was uplifted in fellowship, prayer, praise, and sanctified lives. To be part of such a gathering of consecrated men and women was an inspiration, but as our sailing date was drawing nigh, we had to hurry away to Bolton, where my brother had had to act as my interpreter on a previous occasion, calling in at the Roucan to bid our parents goodbye — for ever, in so far as mother was concerned — and then to Glasgow.

After a round of farewelling at Maxwell Park and a visit to the Scottish Christian Endeavour Convention in Kirkcaldy, where we had a grand time of fellowship, we joined the R.M.S. Kenilworth Castle en route to Cape Town, which had voyaged the round trip to Durban since I left it at Southampton in the meantime.

Before leaving Scotland, I had the pleasure of meeting Dr. and Mrs. Graham, the founders of the St. Andrew's Colonial Homes, Kalimpong, and considered myself fortunate indeed to have had the privilege of conversing with such a saintly, practical couple.

We enjoyed every moment of the voyage, although now quite seasoned voyagers and travellers, and watched, enthralled and interested, Halley's Comet as it raced across the sky with its "Millions of Miles" long blazing tail. The sight was awe-inspiring.

Cape Town, which had just become the legislative capitol of South Africa, Union having come into effect on the 28th of May, 1910, the day we sailed from Southampton, nestling at the bottom of Table Mountain, greeted us with smiles of sunshine, while the Great Colossus of the Ages, Table Mountain, looked benignly down on us two, a happy, contented, loving young couple as we passed through the Gateway of the Southern Continent into South Africa, en route to East London and "Home".

Travelling in a commodious Electric-lit saloon, equipped with steam heating and forming part of a train hauled by a new, large engine ([At the time of writing], 1949, considered very small) we travelled in comfort to our destination, with ample funds to permit of our partaking freely of food in the well-equipped dining car and enjoy the comfort of train beds. The Lord had been good far beyond what we had asked or expected, and we had ample evidence of His promises that if we seek first the Kingdom of Heaven and His righteousness, all these things (the necessaries of life) shall be added.

Oh, what a Saviour is Jesus our Lord.

My Darling soon won the hearts of East London friends by her sweet friendliness, and I took up work in the Sunday School and Christian Endeavour, but did not link up with any other of my previous activities.

Chapter 14
East London

1910–1914

During my absence overseas, the cloud of depression had lifted slightly, union of the provinces had been effected, and an increase in emoluments granted to the long-suffering, much-neglected Railway servants. I received an incremental increase of £12. 0. 0. per annum and was now a married man in receipt of about £192 per annum.

My grading in the service on entering Union was doubtful, owing to the large number of C.S.A.R. men in Johannesburg (now the headquarters of the Railway) who had direct access to the General Manager and Heads of Departments and who were clamouring for the best positions in the new Union grading scheme. Nominally, I was second in charge of the operating office, paying particular attention to the "Accidents" sub-section work.

On New Year's night 19101911, the night passenger train from East London met with a terrible disaster at Gaika Loop, near Cathcart, when 18 passengers and 1 Railway servant were killed and 39 injured, and I was instructed to proceed to the scene immediately. The scene, in a coldish-drizzling rain, was chaotic — nay, it beggared description, and in apportioning out the work to the body of Railwaymen and volunteer workers, I took charge of the work of getting the dead identified and claimed. It was hart-rending, gruesome work, especially in the early morning hours, and after working long hours my assistant broke down completely. Fortunately, I was able to see the work through to completion, working about 3 nights and days without sleep or rest.

This accident brought me into the limelight.

When Mr. W. W. Hoy (subsequently "Sir") required certain information at short notice on the occasion of his visit to East London during 1911, fortunately for me, I was the only person in a position to furnish the data, which I had worked upon for the pleasure of doing so in my leisure moments, who shortly afterwards, when the position of "Trains Clerk" (Senior operating officer) became vacant at East London, selected me for the position over the heads of many claimants who were my senior in the service.

The promotion was quite unexpected as I virtually stepped from the position of a 3rd grade clerk into a grade 1 vacancy with a maximum of £350 per annum. The opposition offered to my appointment was considerable, but it was of the Lord's doing, as humanely speaking, it was not possible to skip a grade, more especially as I had not yet reached the maximum of the one in which I was working. Truly, the Lord was good, having enabled me to place my foot firmly on the first rung of the ladder leading direct to a System Managership.

I became thoroughly acquainted with the whole system during the years 1910-1914 and had my finger on the pulse of the "operating section" around which all railway organization and work hinges. Railway work is "operating", e.g., conveying passengers, parcels, livestock, goods, minerals, etc., the other departments depending for their very existence on "operating".

Our first home was in Fleet Street on the Quigney, and we subsequently transferred to a Railway House. Peggy was kept busy entertaining, visiting, working in the Sunday School, and attending the meetings of the Women's Association in St. George's Church.

We were very happy, surrounded by nice church friends, and when John Andrew (Ian) arrived on the 26th of August, 1911, our cup of blessing was overflowing. When baby was about 7 months old, we spent a holiday in Aliwal North, and at the request of his mother, R. Bein Hagart (now Managing Director of the Anglo-American Corporation, Johannesburg) accompanied us.

On the 20th of January, 1913, our second darling baby son, Mack, arrived, just when our lovely Ian was recovering from a very long, serious illness, having been snatched from the grave in answer to constant, prevailing prayer.

Darling Mum had been wonderfully sustained through the double ordeal by prayer, her own faith, love, courage, resourcefulness, and strength to carry on under almost unbearable circumstances, and was simply marvellous. Through it all she never ceased to look unto Him who bears and answers prayer, and as the sun broke through the dark cloud, we gave thanks to Him whose goodness faileth never.

As I was possibly the youngest officer in charge of a "Section" — operating — in the Union of South Africa, I did not expect to be transferred from East London, at least for several years, but the Lord, who is ever-mindful of His children, knew darling Mum had been called upon to endure almost beyond human strength, and for this reason He spoke to Sir William W. Hoy, General Manager of Railways, and requested him to send me to Port Elizabeth. Even the mighty have to obey His commands and work according to His will.

Chapter 15
Port Elizabeth

1914-1917

All "Great War" years.

A vacancy arose for a "Trains Clerk" at Port Elizabeth, and to the annoyance of the Divisional Superintendent (now System Manager) at East London, who had been a good friend to me and who did not wish to part with me, and the chagrin of the Divisional Superintendent, Port Elizabeth, who had one of his own men in view, the General Manager selected me for the important position.

God was manoeuvring me into position for a subsequent transfer to Pretoria, where I met the officer who insisted that I should be transferred with him to Windhoek, where I was placed in the direct line of becoming a System Manager, and without which transfer I would have never reached that much-coveted position.

We welcomed the climatic change, accepting the railway transfer with quiet assurance that "alles sal reg kom" and it was not long before I was complete master of the position.

Everyone recognised my wide practical and administrative experience, with the result that during my whole term of residence in Port Elizabeth, I was looked upon as the most suitable officer to relieve the two District Inspectors, thus at regular intervals I travelled frequently over the whole system, which extended to De-Aar, Mossel Bay, Graaf Reinet, Somerset East, and Port Alfred.

World War No. 1 commenced on the 4th of August, 1914, quickly followed by minor acts of sabotage, and it fell to my lot to arrange a special train conveying the Prince Alfred Guard Regiment to the Free State. Shipping to and from the port practically ceased, "operating" work was at a standstill, and a spirit of unrest prevailed in the ranks of the staff, but generally speaking they were very loyal.

About 1916, I was promoted to Senior Grade II, which carried a maximum salary of £520 per annum, whilst my actual salary was in the proximity of £430 per annum. The cost of living had advanced by leaps and bounds, a C.O.L.A. [Cost of Living Adjustment] was not paid, and the extra salary scarcely made itself felt in our household, but the increase in my maximum salary opened the way for my transfer to Pretoria at a later date.

War raged with unabating fury on several fronts, German South West Africa soon fell before General [Louis] Botha's victorious troops (the first victory in the Great War), the System Manager and not a few of his satellites did everything in their power to make things difficult for me, the Powers of Evil tried to destroy me in several accidents, and generally railway life was not easy, but blessed be His name the Lord sustained and strengthened me in all my ways.

What of our home life — first in Havelock Street, then Mackie Street, and to finish in Port Elizabeth in a beautifully situated house overlooking the harbour from the shore and over the bay, where we could see ships entering and leaving the harbour, was truly magnificent. It was near this house that the Royal Train was stabled in 1947 when the King expressed himself freely in regard to the wonderful site which had been chosen. We were happy, with Christ in charge, and when on the 2nd of September, 1915, our dear, sweet Harold (Mousie) arrived in our home, we were overjoyed. Coming in a war, a child of God in whom reigned the spirit of the Lord from childhood years, he left us in war. His sweet, gentle, keen intellect having made an impression on our hearts and home which will never be effaced.

Just before war was declared, my darling was taken to hospital, suffering from a sudden, painful attack of Renal Colic, but God, answering our earnest, prevailing prayer, enabled the doctor to remove the obstruction without resorting to surgery.

We were very happy in the Hill Presbyterian Church where the Rev. James McRobert and his active, beautiful wife exercised a powerful ministry, but Presbyterian like two sermons weekly represented the church's activities, apart from the Sunday School and the Bible Class, which I taught.

Mum was a member of the Women's Association, I was a Sunday School teacher and Assistant Scoutmaster of the Hill Troop, and our darling two fine, little boys attended the Kindergarten Sunday School.

During 1916, Ian commenced attending a Kindergarten weekday school conducted by Miss Duncan, a cousin of Sir Patrick Duncan, who became Governor General of the Union of South Africa.

Their Excellencies, the Governor General and Viscountess Buxton visited Port Elizabet during our residence there, and the arranging of their journey, which was all by rail, was undertaken by myself and staff.

During our first few years in Port Elizabeth, we spent a holiday at Oudtshoorn where I took the opportunity of visiting the Cango Caves, and during 1916, my darling together with the three babies spent a holiday at Rosmead when, feeling lonely without my loved ones, I penned the following lines as an appendix to a letter:

> Return Oh wanderer to thy home,
> Thy Daddy calls Thee yet,
> No longer now at Rosmead roam
> On holiday my Pet.
> Return — Return
> Return Oh Darling to Thy home,
> Thy Daddy calls for Thee,
> My spirit and my words say "come",
> Oh now from Rosmead flee.
> Return — Return

Our days at Port Elizabeth were fast drawing to a close, although Mum and I were quite unconscious of the fact, and when the System Manager informed m that I had been selected by the General Manager for transfer to Pretoria, I was delightfully surprised, and Mum shared fully in joyful expectation.

We enjoyed our short stay in Port Elizabeth with its bracing seaside climate, lovely Humewood, the Donkin Reserve, the well-kept park and the friendliness of the people, although as usual I did not make permanent friends, but my Darling Mum, who has always had a great capacity for making and keeping friends, made up, if that were possible, for my shortcomings.

I had enjoyed every moment of my railway life, notwithstanding the opposition of the System Manager and some of the staff, which apart from our home and Sunday School, was my sole interest, although the System did not grip my very heartstrings as the "Eastern" (East London) had done. That of course was natural, seeing East London was my first love.

> With Christ I walk on loft heights,
> And clear pure air inhale,
> The Lord himself my Guiding Light
> His love shall never fail.
> J.R.
> Windhoek, 1940

Mr. and Mrs. J. Rogan with Family

L to R: Ian, Harold, Douglas, and Mack

(Taken in Pretoria)

Mr. and Mrs. J. Rogan with Family

L to R: Ian, Douglas, Harold, Mack

(Taken in Windhoek S.W.A.)

Chapter 16
Pretoria

1917-1923

Bewildered with many trains passing to and fro, the endless stream of passengers hurrying to and fro, and crowds of raw-blanket natives, we waited at Germiston for the Pretoria connection to arrive from Johannesburg, and as the train sped quickly over the High Veld, we fell in love with the greenness of the veld, the decorative clumps of Cosmos, and looked excitedly towards the residence of General Smuts, whose name was even then a household word in South Africa and Britain.

Travelling down the Fountains Valley, we marvelled at the richness of the scenery and hailed our first view of the Union Buildings with delight, even though it was only momentary. I had seen them previously, shortly after the foundations were laid, when on a business trip from East London, after Union.

The large station with its 7 platforms, several trains arriving and leaving simultaneously, two signal cabins, and more people than I had at any time seen in East London and Port Elizabeth station, crested in me a feeling of justifiable pride and a sense of advancement in the service of the railways.

My salary was £440 per annum with a C.O.L. allowance, and my position was that of Senior Operating Officer in the Senior II Grade, designated "Trains Clerk" — now (1949) Assistant Superintendent — Operating.

I was received without reservation by the System Manager and the senior officers, who were all very kind and helpful to me, but from the commencement I was conscious of an undercurrent of opposition in certain directions, not unconnected, I had reason to believe, with the S.O.E. Society (I was Scotch), the Free Masons, and subsequently from the direction of the Railway Institute.

In business, everyone was very nice and cooperative, but the warning I received from a high official source to be on my guard was very helpful indeed.

The war was at its height, the demand was for the delivery of coal and still more coal at Lourenço Marques was insistent, and with depleted staff due to recruitment, insufficiently powerful engines that were much in need of repair, lack of rolling stock, and inadequate track space, the staff responded loyally and marvellously to the demand. Men worked long hours cooperatively, Sunday was ruled out as a day of rest. As a matter of fact, it became the busiest day of the week, the wheels were kept turning and the loads were delivered. I worked an average of about 12 hours daily, the running staff worked many more hours than was good for them, and when peace came, we were all mentally and physically finished. At this time, a word of encouragement or praise from headquarters would have gone a long way to restoring our shattered nervous systems — but — no doubt the men at Headquarters had also been overworked and also needed encouragement, which most of them got in the shape of promotion or an increase in salary.

My services were used to relieve the two District Inspectors whenever necessary, and this welcome respite and breather in the open country twice yearly, kept me going, as it is certain the constant strain of work and long hours without a break would have proved too much for me. Thus I became intimately acquainted with the whole large system extending from the Limpopo to the Komati River at Komati Poort, Piet Retief, Rustenberg, Vaalwater, Settler (afterwards Tuinplaats), and down the Solati Line, part of which passed through the game reserve.

In March 1922, during the Labour upheaval on the Rand, I was required to be on duty night and day, sleeping or resting in the offices when possible, being supplied with a Military Pass during the period when Martial Law was in force.

Our home was a happy one with Jesus in full control as its acknowledged head and in all our ways. We loved Him with ever-increasing fervour, and our darling boys had a realistic view of His peace in our home and lives, whose mercies were new every morning, with His guiding hand directing us in all our ways.

On the 25th of October, 1919, our darling fourth son, Douglas, was born, when we all rejoiced and gave thanks to God who had been so gracious to my darling Mum. The three little boys — Ian was only 8 years old — were delighted and selected the name "Douglas" for their little brother.

The slaughter of the world's manhood in world war No. 1 came to an end with the defeat of the Germans on the Western front, and on the 11th of November, 1919, the first Armistice Day was observed when the King called the people of Britain and of the Commonwealth to observe a two-minute silence in remembrance of the glorious dead whose name liveth forever.

During 1916, whilst the soldiers were still in the trenches, an epidemic called "Spanish Flu" swept over the whole world and millions died. In Pretoria, death appeared on every hand, young and old being taken away indiscriminately, but the dread plague, for such it was, appeared to be most virulent amongst strong, healthy Europeans and Coloured persons, the death troll amongst the latter in Cape Town and Kimberly being dreadful.

During November, 1920, my darling Mum was taken to the Pretoria General Hospital with a serious internal complaint, where she underwent an operation for appendicitis and other complications. It was an anxious time, and distressing when, at about 2 O'clock in the morning, there were practically no signs of life. But again, prevailing, earnest, beseeching prayer prevailed, and throughout the day, life returned, although very gradually.

Whilst residing in Pretoria, we spent a lovely holiday in Mossel Bay, where the bracing climate, fine swimming, and lovely surroundings were much enjoyed by us all, Ian and Mack especially being like little fish in the swimming pool. Mum and the three boys (before the birth of Douglas) also spent a nice holiday in East London, where Mum renewed many old friendships.

St. Andrew's Pretoria, with the Rev. E. MacMillan (subsequently Dr.) in charge, was our spiritual home, but on the whole, there was very little spiritual fellowship — the church was no different from the other

Presbyterian churches with which we were associated during our transferring years, being luke-warm, and money-minded to the exclusion of all else.

I was Superintendent of the Presbyterian Sunday School, and during March of 1922, I was appointed an Elder in St. Andrew's, being then 41 years of age. It was a great honour to one considered comparatively young for eldership, where generally only men well advanced in years were ordained.

Our children being very small, Mum did not take any part in the Women's Association, but faithfully attended the church whenever it was possible to do so.

On one occasion, I was the leader in a combined meeting of Sunday Schools when I spoke on the subject "Are we teaching on right Lines".

We loved Pretoria, where we bought a house in Buiten Street, after living near to "Jess's" Cottage of Rider Hagard fame, in Rider Hagard Street, the little boys were happy and loveable, and we had gathered around our home a nice circle of friends. The rose gardens, flowers, bougainvillea, golden shower, Union Buildings, Fountains Valley, and the stately church square became part of our lives, whilst the Transvaal, with its expansive High and Low velds, rivers, mountains, and krantz, became very dear to us.

But the road to System Managership led via Pretoria only and quite unexpectedly, but under the guiding hand of our Heavenly Father I was selected to fill the position of Chief Clerk in the office of System Manager, Windhoek, South West Africa, Mandated Territory.

Unfortunately, my selection for the much-coveted position caused much resentment as, being in the Senior II Grade, with a salary of £520 per annum, it was necessary for me to jump over the men in the Senior I positions who were at the time in receipt of salaries in excess of mine.

In 1923, we said "totsiens" to Pretoria, for such it proved to be, and left behind puerile opposition on the part of a few who did not agree with my open hostility towards the "Bar" of the Railway Institute, and others who envied my promotion as I was younger than some of them, whilst the great majority acknowledged my experience and ability as a railwayman and my fearlessness as a follower of the Lord Jesus Christ.

Chapter 17
Windhoek, South West Africa (Mandated Territory)

1927-1927

Chief Clerk, Windhoek, at a maximum salary of £600. 0. 0. per annum.

It's a long, long way to Windhoek, and little did we think when we said goodbye to our friends in Pretoria that we were commencing a journey which would last for 40 days and nights, that we would have to travel part of the train journey in trucks and voyage by ship Lüderitz to Walvis Bay.

On arrival at De Aar, we were advised to make ourselves comfortable in the hotel, as it was uncertain when we would be able to proceed due to washaways at Putsonder water, and after about a two-day wait at that busy junction, we proceeded on our 882-mile journey to Windhoek.

Crossing over the Low-Level Bridge spanning the Grange River at Upington, it was entirely covered by water with only the rails showing now and then in the lapping of the water, and the border at Nakop was crossed in brilliant sunshine. It was here where the first shot fired by a German soldier in the S.W.A. campaign killed a Union policeman, the incident giving rise to the rumour that the Germans were attacking the Union from S.W.A.

From Nakop onwards, the world was in all respects an entirely different one in which time was of no account, everybody seemed to live in a carefree and easy manner, the railways used old, discarded Union engines, and small Union trucks intermixed with old, dilapidated German stock, whilst the bare, sandy, stony veld contrasted unfavourable with the Transvaal High Veld.

The natives were few in number and the scattered Europeans looked lonely and inactive.

On the arrival of the train at Keetmanshoop, we were informed that extensive washaways had occurred to the North, but no one seemed to know just how extensive, the rumour being that whole miles of railway had disappeared, and this actually proved to be the case.

Under atrocious conditions and almost unbearable heat, we lived in the train, alternating to the hotel in the Dorp and an empty house for about three long, dreary weeks, always hoping that we would be able to continue our journey on the morrow, but we didn't.

Food was scare and what was procurable was of inferior quality, water for bathing was not available and very doubtful for drinking. We nevertheless contrived to enjoy ourselves, and Mum's management in the circumstances was just too wonderful for words. Only my darling could have managed to pull through safely under such circumstances with 4 lively boys to care for and to look after.

Our loving Father had arranged our transfer to Windhoek, of that we were certain, and nothing, not even extensive washaways, could prevent us from getting there in His own good time.

At long last after it was seen the position was hopeless, at least for the immediate future, we were instructed to travel via Seeheim Junction to Lüderitz, where we would be able to take a ship to Walvis Bay and a train via Swakopmund to Windhoek. Therefore, in high hopes we set out on the second stage of our journey, fortunately unconscious of the risks, hardships, and hunger immediately ahead of us. On reaching Seeheim, we found ourselves involved in another washaway, which entailed a day or two's delay, with food almost unprocurable, and further on at Sandverhaar, we had to again detrain, owing to a culvert having been washed away, and cross a narrow, strong-flowing, deep stream on a single-sleeper bridge. This was a nerve-wracking, dangerous experience undertaken in the darkness of mid-night, but Mum was courageous — more so than I was, and the boys were not old enough to realise the risk taken.

But the most terrifying experience was yet to come, when descending the Aus Mountain approaching the Garum Valley, where, owing to a defect in the engine, the driver lost control of the train, and we rushed at high speed, hid in a cloud of sand, towards the far away valley. It was only by the goodness of God that the engine and train did not overturn, or at least leave the rails and plunge into the veld.

The whole journey from Sandverhaar in cattle trucks and the guards van (we were in the latter vehicle) was a dreadful nightmare, accompanied by hunger, thirst, and aching bones as a result of the hard floor on which we had to sit and lie. The Namib Desert never looked so dismal, never in our experience was there such a long night, and never was the sea such a welcome sight.

Wind-swept Lüderitz, in the Namib Desert, streets deep in sand, no fresh water, and [evaporated and] condensed sea water retailed by the railways at a price which made imported German beer appear cheap. German-built houses of solid stone, large railway and government buildings, and a small, sheltered harbour would at other times have been of interest, but we were travel-weary, looking anxiously towards the entrance to the harbour for the promised ship.

The S.S. Sultan carried a deck cargo of wild animals, and from Lüderitz to Walvis Bay, every nook and corner of the small German vessel was crowded with over 130 stranded rail passengers, many of whom had reached dire financial straits.

We were fixed up comfortably in an Officers Cabin, and after an uneventful voyage, we reached Walvis Bay where, to our consternation, we were informed that the Swakop River Bridge, 20 miles to the North on the Main Line to Windhoek, had been washed away and that the passenger accommodation intended for us could not be got through to Walvis Bay.

After travelling in cattle trucks to the wrecked bridge and covered rails with bordering sand dunes and windswept sand slashing our faces, we crossed the river, women and children in donkey wagons whilst the men waded thigh deep.

We spent the night in the doldrums at Swakopmund (where the Germans had made a jetty) after surmounting incredible difficulties at enormous cost, and in the morning, we learned with a feeling akin to horror that our train was held up further north at Okshandja, some 150 miles distant, due to a washaway. We could do nothing but wait, and we filled in the time looking at the sights of this predominately German town.

After a day or two, our pent-up feelings were let loose in great excitement when we saw our train approaching Swakopmund enveloped in a cloud of desert sand, hauled by an ancient, dilapidated, ex-German engine.

The System Manager had very thoughtfully sent his fully equipped private saloon with attendant "Jackson" in charge, for our accommodation, and from the arrival of the train until our arrival in Windhoek, we were under the friendly but critical cynosure of the other weary washaway passengers.

Travelling through the Namib during the night, we reached Windhoek in the late forenoon of the following day, after an eventful journey of 40 days and 40 nights (which under normal circumstances could have been accomplished in 3 days of railway travel), which we enjoyed in spite of heat, rain, hunger, thirst, discomfort, risk, and the everlasting sand. Our arrival in Windhoek coincided with my 42nd birthday.

Throughout the journey, Mum was perfectly marvellous, calm, resourceful, and courageous, and we found pleasure in everything as it came along, having decided to treat the journey as a picnic; and it was no picnic!

The saloon No. 17 in which we travelled so luxuriously from Swakopmund was the vehicle which the Nederlands Government presented to the late Paul Kruger, President of the Transvaal Republic when the railways in the Transvaal and the O.F.S. were known as the Z.A.S.M. [Nederlandsche Zuid-Afrikaansche Spoorwegmaatschappij — NetherlandsSouth African Railway Company].

Windhoek — so this was Windhoek, the idol of the Germans before World War No. 1, and the centre of their dreams for future colonial expansion under the Nazi regime, with its German-named streets, German residences in Lietwein, and other streets mostly occupied by civil servants and railwaymen, massive, cumbersome, German telephone instruments, double-headed eagles everywhere, Hereros who remembered the massacre of their people during the trumped-up Herero rebellion of 1905, German "Beer" gardens, open 7 days weekly, and book shops stocked with German books and literature. Notwithstanding the foreign atmosphere, we loved the place from the moment of our arrival and were soon comfortably settled in a large, lovely railway house that had been specially reserved for our accommodation.

I was next to the System Manager in seniority on the non-technical side of the office, and my first requirement was to adjust myself to the slowness of the office pace after the rushing tempo of the war years in Pretoria. This presented, curious as it may seem, a real problem to me, and it was sometime before I could comfortably realise that "more is nog 'n dag".

Everything and everybody was slow-moving on the S.W.A. railway system, and discipline was not enforced as it was in the Union. Many of the staff were inclined to take undue liberties under the benign local management, but on the whole, they were a fine body of men, even if somewhat inexperienced generally.

Engines, rolling stock, and buildings were to a great extent ex-German, and we were allowed the use of ex-German, solidly made oak furniture in our houses with preponderatingly German populations in Windhoek, Keetmanshoof, Lüderitz, Usakos, Swakopmund, and a host of smaller places, who on the whole were friendly if somewhat sullen.

The No. 1, S.W.A., private saloon allocated to me was specially built for the comfort, convenience, and enjoyment of the Crown Prince of German, whose tour of S.W.A., then one of Germany's much-treasured possessions, had to be postponed on account of the outbreak of World War No. 1.

Likewise, the large, narrow-gauge motor trolley, built for the Crown Prince's tour over the northern section of the territory, was also available for my use. It was the finest, fastest, and largest NG motor trolley I have ever seen.

I travelled at intervals over the whole system, necessitating 3,552 miles return journey, travelling over one section at a time, and in a sense I got used to the slowness of travel, distances, loneliness, sand, and sand storms in the terrifying Namib Desert that encroaches far inland in its long stretch from North to South.

Walvis Bay, situated in the midst of desert desolation, was just emerging from isolation , Lüderitz was thoroughly German, holding at arms length as far as possible the inevitable encroachment of Union Nationals and Officials.

In the far north, everything and everyone was predominately German, and were not reconciled to the idea that S.W.A. was Mandated Territory and that they were no longer controlled from Berlin.

I travelled in my coach with passenger and goods trains and by rail motor drenched with sand, sun-baked, wind-swept, and in rain to Swakopmund, Walvis Bay, Usakos — Tsumeb — Grootfontein, Outjo, Keetmanshoof, Lüderitz, and Upington and De Aar, saw wild game of many kinds, of which the koodoo was the largest, and on several occasions got help up in washaways, but never again for 40 days.

Even the uncomfortable travel was enjoyable, and valuable experience was gained for the day when I would be System Manager of the system.

During 1923, I accompanied General B.C. Hertzog, Prime Minister of the Union of South Africa, when he toured S.W.A. by special train and rail car and lunched with him and Mr. Grys Hofmeyer, Administrator of S.W.A. in the private saloon. A charming gentleman, in whose company I was made to feel at ease, and I consider it a great honour to have lunched with him.

The Wit and Swart Nosof Rivers in flood, especially at their confluence, sunsets, as seen from the hill behind our house in Windhoek and in the desert, the high-spouting artesian wells in the midst of the dry and thirsty land east of Marienthal, the everlasting sand dunes, barren and desolate, and a wind storm at Lüderitz, when sand clouds darkened the air were impressive, inspiring sights.

I visited the lighthouses at Swakopmund, Walvis Bay (Pelican Point), and Lüderitz. The crayfish industry, Lüderitz, was interesting, the flocks of beautiful flamingos at Walvis Bay, especially when on the wing, presented a wonderful sight, and in the far North, I saw a real Bushman whose appearance was scarcely human, who had just been captured in the Kalahari Desert, with a small, twisted body, small, beady eyes, and high cheekbones.

Passing through Rehoboth during the rebellion, where aeroplanes under Sir Pierre van Rynveld, had just made a demonstration over the dorp, I could see no signs of hostilities or of insubordination. The affair appeared to have been staged in the administrative offices at Windhoek, and it was subsequently stated in the Union Parliament that "Rebellion" existed in the minds of certain high-placed Government officials.

On our return from a visit to Scotland (see Chapter XIX), we received a very warm welcome from our circle of friends, and I was soon immersed in railway work of an easy-going description, but nevertheless essential.

But the path along which my Heavenly Father was leading me towards System Managership went far afield via devious ways, although I knew it not at the time, but Mum and I never doubted but that the ultimate end would be to His glory and to our satisfaction. In this spirit we received the news that I was being re-transferred to Pretoria, where I had been appointed District Inspector of the Northern Section of the System.

He leadeth me: O blessed thought!
O words with heavenly comfort fraught!
Whate'er I do, where'er I be,
Still 'tis God's hand that leadeth me.
Hymn No. 625
The Church Hymnary (1893)

We enjoyed our sojourn in Windhoek, the wide, lovely expanses were my friends when travelling alone in my coach, in spite of the civil service snobbery, for the reason that our Redeemed lives were "In Christ" kept joyfully and peacefully by His power.

Spiritually, we had passed through a time of testing in a dry and barren land without a live church connection, having had to lean heavily on Him without and Christian fellowship.

Christ was very precious and ever near to us, and with Him, we did not need nor want worldly fellowship with its accompanying doubtful social life.

The Windhoek Advertiser

12th of January, 1927

Railway Presentation

> The Railway Staff assembled in the Railway Board Room on Friday 7th of January to show their respect and esteem for Mr. J. Rogan, who has so ably filled the position of Chief Clerk for S.W.A. Division for over three years and who has now been transferred to Pretoria.
> Mr. Wallis, Divisional Superintendent, who presided, commented on the tribute paid to Mr. Rogan's popularity by the large and representative gathering in the room.
> The whole staff on the Division respected Mr. Rogan. . ..he is going to a centre where his energy and abilities will have fuller scope.. . .Mr. Wallis asked Mr. Rogan to accept a handsome cheque.
> Prior to departure from Windhoek Mrs. Wallis entertained Mrs. Rogan and her friends to tea and during the afternoon presented her with a handsome handbag and a suit case subscribed to by S.W.A. ladies. . .

What of our home life in this far away outpost of the Empire in the midst of a population 2/3 German, whose main hobby seemed to be beer drinking in the Gardens (really squares with shrubs) of the hotels, but who nevertheless were a sober, industrious, quiet people, not yet caught in the vortex of nazi-ism.

The social life in the community was not for us as the civil servants, who were in the majority in so far as the "British" population was concerned, held everything and everybody belonging to the railway at arms length, and the few scattered members of the Wesleyan Church Community (there was no church building) did not appear to have sufficient life in them to create a truly spiritual atmosphere. This is not to be wondered at, seeing they were few in number, and with its continental atmosphere, Windhoek was in every respect spiritually dead.

My darling Mum and I collected a few friends who had found the Lord, and from time to time we had fellowship meetings which were truly times of soul refreshing in our home.

Our lovely boys attended the boys' school where they made satisfactory progress, and when we decided to go overseas, we sent Ian and Mack to Dale College, King William's Town, where they resided in the Presbyterian Hostel. To reach the school from Windhoek, they had to travel approximately 1500 miles in each direction, occupying about 5 days of journeying.

During 1924, we spent a nice holiday in East London, renewing old friendships and enjoying the fellowships of St. George's Church, where the congregation was ministered unto by Dr. Douglas, the Rev. Geo. Blair having returned to Scotland.

I preached once or twice in the Wesleyan Church service, which was held in the Won Hall, but did not work in the Sunday School where our little boys were faithful scholars.

So time, as always when there is love at home, flew past quickly, smoothly, and sweetly in an atmosphere of deep, restful, spiritual content. It could not be otherwise with Christ at the head of our home, my Angel Mum in charge, and four lovely, obedient boys romping about.

I have found a friend in Jesus
He's everything to me
He's the fairest of ten thousand to my soul
He's the lily of the valley,
In Him alone I see,
All I need to make and keep me fully whole.

Chapter 18
Scotland Revisited

1925

With Ian and Mack comfortably settled in the Presbyterian Church Hostel and attending Dale College, King William's Town, Mum, Harold, Douglas, and myself left Windhoek in my private saloon en route to Walvis Bay where we joined the S.S. Tanganyika during May en route to Scotland. The voyage was very pleasant, notwithstanding that the crew and the great majority of the passengers were Germans, and after calling at Lobito Bay, Benguela (an extremely beautiful place), Tenerife, and Lisbon, we disembarked at Southampton to the strains of Scotch airs finishing up with "Will ye no come back again" played by the ship's band.

Nearing Lisbon, we passed through a large fishing fleet of sailing ships — a lovely sight in the early morning sun.

After a few days in London, during which time we spent some time in the Wembly World's Exhibition, we travelled by express train to Glasgow where we were warmly received by Mr. & Mrs. Smith — Peggy's father and mother — Mr. Smith then being a retired railwayman after 50 years of service, enjoying peace and happiness as the just rewards of a well-spent life.

Everything was changed, especially Maxwell Park and the Station House, where we were strangers and merely passengers in the crowd. The passengers whom we knew and respected were now unknown to us, the lads looked odd and even clumsy in their heavy corduroy suits, and the smartness of the foreman's blue uniform had lost its appeal to me. I prayed that these lads would get the "kick" out of their work and in wearing the uniform that had been mine 25 years previously.

Whilst at Wembly, we dined in the S.A.R.&H. dining car, where specially prepared South African food was served by S.A.R. dining car stewards, and the car, with a brass plate affixed to indicate its association with Wembley, is still in service in the Union (1949).

The Roucan was still a quiet, sleepy, and interesting place, but motor cars were seen occasionally passing through the village at speed. We were total strangers, even at the church on Sunday, where it was seen that young men of my youthful days had grown old before their time, and old folks had passed on. We spent most of our limited time in and around Dumfries, the Queen of the South, rowing up the River Nith and visiting the many beautiful places in the neighbourhood.

Our next place to stay was in the West Highlands at Tighnabruaich — on the Kyles of Bute — and from there we travelled to Inverness, the prettiest town we have ever seen, where we met, by chance, Dr. & Mrs. MacMillan of Pretoria.

Whilst in Inverness, we visited Colloden Moor, where Bonnie Prince Charlie and his loyal, half-starved, and poorly equipped Highlanders, who shook the British throne to its foundations in 1746, were disastrously defeated by the Duke of Cumberland's troops. The mounds in which the clansmen are buried, with one mound for the English soldiers, are still plainly seen. This was the last battle (16th of April, 1746) ever fought on British soil.

Calling in at Edinburgh, we visited many well-remembered places, and enjoyed seeing Princes Street again, with its magnificent gardens and stately monuments.

Farewell to Glasgow and to our people there, the Roucan, where father was living in the old home cared for by a granddaughter, mother having passed on, Bolton, where my brother and his family reside, and where I had had language difficulties on the occasion of my first visit there, soon followed, and once again, we found ourselves London, where we saw the Prince of Wales, accompanied by the King and other royalty, passing through Trafalgar Square, the Prince being on his way back from his tour of South Africa.

Seven years had passed since the termination of World War No. 1, when Britain lost the cream of her manhood on battlefields all over the world, and South Africa, under the bold leadership of General Louis Botha, had also given freely of her sons and material. Nevertheless, the people with whom we conversed never mentioned war, nor made reference to the Union's voluntary effort on the side of the Allies. Sport and holidaying seemed to monopolise their lives, with the church and spiritual matters entirely eliminated from what appeared to be a somewhat circumscribed manner of living.

Mum and I, with the exception of our contacts with relations, were living in a foreign land, although we spoke the same language, and it appeared to us that we belonged to a newer, better, and happier world, where the sun shines and people look prosperous, even though such may not be the case.

Harold and Douglas were much admired, our darling Harold entertaining people with sweet little Afrikaans recitations, but, like myself when young, they had English language difficulties, only this time it was with the "broad" speaking Scotch children.

The homeward-bound voyage on board the S.S. Ussukuma was uneventful, except for the fact that the engines broke down in a rough sea in the Bay of Biscay, when the ship developed an unpleasant side-on roll that caused most of the passengers (including myself for the first and last time) to go down with seasickness.

Opposite Swakopmund, the rising sun bathed the sand dunes in shining gold, and we lifted our hearts in praise to our Heavenly Father, giving Him thanks for a pleasant, memorable, and happy holiday amidst scenes forever dear to us. He had indeed dealt bountifully with us, prospering us in all our ways, and brought us safely "Home" to our beloved South Africa. What though the green fields, lofty Bens, rivers, lakes, and cities had been left behind, and now we saw only sand dunes stretching far inland, this was South Africa, our "home", and as we stepped ashore at Walvis Bay, we laughed for joy, our hearts and lives being in tune with this, our beloved land.

Breathes there a man with soul so dead who never
to himself hath said This is my own, my native land?
Breathes There the Man
Sir Walter Scott (1805)

There were no washaways on the line, the newly constructed
Swakopmund Bridge stood firm (it collapsed a few years later), and
we travelled uninterruptedly in comfort to Windhoek, where we were
immediately welcomed by a small but enthusiastic band of Christian friends.

In the intervening two years (1925-1927) I travelled a great deal
over the line from De Aar to Walvis Bay, Lüderitz, Keimoes, Usakos —
Tsumeb — Grootfontein, and Outjo.

On one occasion, I saw a swarm of voetgangers [immature locusts], the
extent and density of which was such as to be indescribable, having to be
seen to be appreciated. Their movements and climbing in the long grass
produced motion resembling the waves of the sea.

I passed through sand storms in the Kolmans Kop District of such
density that visibility was restricted to a matter of yards.

The Orange River, in a record flood which I understand has never been
surpassed, was an awe-inspiring sight as it flowed with mighty, irresistible
force, leaping over the Augrabies Falls (also called King George) west of
Kakamas in its journey towards the South Atlantic Ocean.

The Police camel desert patrols, penetrating into the Kalahari desert east
of Gobabis, the artesian wells of which there were several east of Marienthal
in the heart of desert land, were such a source of interest, and what was left
of the Herero people slaughtered by the ruthless Germans in their savage
campaign to obliterate these cattle-rearing-minded natives, could only be
looked upon with a feeling of intense sympathy. Incidentally, the women
of this tribe are invariably taller than the men, being mostly over 5'10" in
height, and with coloured doek of 812 inches posed on their heads they
looked like walking lampposts.

God works in a mysterious way, and to enable me to become System
Manager at Windhoek, I had to return to Pretoria, work in Johannesburg,
Kimberly, and again Pretoria and Johannesburg to end my official career
at Windhoek.

My salary was £600 per annum.

The Rogan Family

Pretoria, ~1929

Front: Douglas

Back, L. to R.: John, Andrew (Ian), Harold.

Chapter 19
Pretoria

1927-1934

Thes were the most varied years in all my railway service and in a way the most interesting.

I was now District Inspector, Pretoria, at a salary of £600 per annum, supervising the North Eastern District of the Transvaal Railway System, extending from Witbank through Pretoria and Petersburg to Messina (Beit Bridge over the Limpopo was then being built), Soekmekaar, the Selati Line running through a portion of the game reserve to Komati Poort, Cullinan, Rustenberg, Tuinplaats, and Roberts Heights branch lines. It was a long, busy section, demanding constant movement with Enquiries of Investigation, Disciplinary Enquiries (distasteful things), and staff matters engaging much of my attention. Unfortunately, I had to sacrifice my much-beloved happy home life, leaving my darling Mum to manage the home with four active boys who should have been enjoying my companionship and help. At weekends, I was too tired to thoroughly enjoy home and the constant travelling over long distances created a feeling of unsettledness. Nevertheless, I was happy in my work, the outside staff cooperated loyally, and not a few gratuitously acknowledged my intimate knowledge of the various spheres of station and operating work.

Ian and Mack, much to their dislike, were brought home from Dale College to attend Pretoria Boys High School, whilst Harold and Douglas were students at Sunnyside Secondary School.

I was installed as Sunday School Superintendent of St. Columba's Hatfield, where we were living at the time, but on the arrival of the Rev. Peter Gordon, M.A., now Minister of the St. Mark's Church, Yeoville,

Johannesburg (1949), I took over the Superintendentship of the Presbyterian Railway Sunday School for the second time.

During February, 1927, I was restored to the position of "Elder" in St. Andrew's Church, in the same year Mum was Vice-President of the Women's Association, which she represented at the Kimberly General Assembly during 1929.

During 19271934, the whole family was engaged in the Good Hope Mission work carried on by a band of enthusiastic workers amongst the "poor whites" in the suburb of that name. We were a happy band, and with four boys in the work, for which we continually gave praise to God, our home was the centre of meeting for young people who enjoyed the fellowship, laughter, and fun.

I relieved the Station Master, Pretoria, for ten months, when it was necessary for me to contact cabinet ministers and others of High Rank. In conversations with Mr. Patrick Duncan, afterwards "Sir" and Governor General of the Union, he told me that in the event of the station becoming vacant, I would not get the appointment as I had not the right name for such an appointment.

I conversed at times with Generals Hertzog and Kemp, Mr. Piet Grobbelaar (a great Nationalist and nephew of the late President Paul Kruger), Mr. Havenga, Harm Oost, and Jan Hofmeyer, who died last year (1948). They were all pleasant and easy of approach.

Having contracted Malaria fever whilst on the Low Veld, I asked to be taken off the road, and when finished relieving, I was appointed Senior General, Rates and Claims Clerk (Commercial section of the System Office) during 1929. The work was interesting and presented no difficulties to me.

During 1928, I passed the Railway Examination in Afrikaans as prescribed by the Government Educational Department, and after a short period in the Commercial Section of the System Office, I was transferred, much against my inclination, to the position of Chief Clerk in the office of the Stores Superintendent, Pretoria, at a salary of £630 p.a.

Looking back on that unwanted transfer, it is difficult to believe that one's fellowmen could be so bitterly hostile to an appointment to which they strongly objected on the grounds that I was an "outsider". They did not know me, nor had any of them every seen me, but the fact that I, from another Department, had been given the appointment in preference to one of the Stores Officers was sufficient in their estimation to let loose much violent resentment and obstructive working. But the Lord sustained me, notwithstanding that the resentment resulted in my breaking a wrist, and through their withholding all work from me, I was able to devote much time daily to the study of Stores accounting, organisation, management, and Executive work. Consequently, when the Stores Superintendent proceeded on pension during 1933, I stepped into the vacancy, to the chagrin of my persecutors. They need not have feared, however, for, like Joseph when his guilty brethren went to him for assistance, I was able to recognise the hand of the Lord in sending me to the Stores Department. In my unexpected promotion, grace was given to me to treat everyone with justice and brotherly kindness.

I enjoyed my new post very much, with its many ramifications, and business visits to the Depots at Germiston, Klerksdorp, Waterval Boven, and Witbank.

I now ranked equal to an Assistant Superintendent (operating), but my heart was in "Transportation", and I prayed for, and expectantly looked towards, the day when I would again be in "Operating", notwithstanding the constant demands that work in that important section of railway work made on one's time, mental capacity, and physical energy.

Stores work moved along an even surface, with no necessity for hustle, and Stores Department men could not, in my opinion, be classified or graded as Railwaymen, any more than the Catering staff.

My salary was £700 p.a., with a maximum salary of £750 p.a.

When I was leaving the Stores Department, the men who had bitterly opposed my appointment as Chief Clerk presented me with a gold fountain pen and pencil and said some very complimentary things about me.

Chapter 20
Kimberly

1934-1935

*B*ehold what great things the Lord hath done.

The year 1934 will always find a nice place in our memories, for during this eventful year, when holidaying at Scottburgh, darling Mum ran towards the side of the waves, where I was bathing, waving a telegram and calling out "we are not at Pretoria — we are at Kimberly", and sure enough we were. The telegram was an instruction to me to proceed to Kimberly immediately to relieve the Superintendent (Commercial and Operating), and in a few days, I was in Kimberly.

Mum, Harold, and Douglas remained in Scottburgh to complete their holiday, where Mum and I were House Father and Mother, and Harold and Douglas were workers, in the Special Seaside Mission (S.S.M.), and subsequently they returned to Pretoria, where they remained for the time being.

The Kimberly System extends from De Aar Kimberly to Bulawayo, Kimberly to Klerksdorp (where I had a Stores Depot), Barkley West, Pudimoe – Coligny – Welwerdiend. Belmont – Douglas, with very extensive Road Motor Services operating in all directions.

During my extensive travels, I visited the Moffatt Mission Church in Kurumen, of which mention is made in the life of Robert Moffatt, the Pioneer Missionary to the Bechuanas, who settled in this (then) very isolated and wild part of Africa during 1817, as follows, viz:

> "By this journey (1835) which occupied 3 months, the way was paved for some American Missionaries to reside with Moselekatze and the country was surveyed to find timber for the roof of the new (kuruman) church . . . timber was afterwards collected by Messrs. Hamilton and Edwards and fashioned into the roof of the church, which stands to this day"

and it still stands (1949), a monument to faith, perseverance, courage, and hard work.

The garden where David Livingstone wooed Mary Moffat was visited, the rushing stream of cool, clear water out of the hillside, used by Robert and Mary Moffatt, their daughter Mary, David Livingstone, and other notable missionaries were all very interesting.

After the lapse of over a hundred years, the buildings and surroundings still speak eloquently of the laborious sacrificial labours of these devoted servants of the Lord, amongst the heathen Beckwanas (as spelt by Robert Moffatt) in darkest Africa.

Of Pitsani, in Bechuanaland, which I passed through on several occasions, it is recorded in the Biography of Robert Moffatt:

> " . . . visited Pitsana where a great concourse of natives had gathered, consisting of different sections of the Barolong tribe, who had been driven out of their country the previous year during the invasion of the Mantatese".

Pitsani was the place where Dr. Jameson, of Jameson Raid fame, assembled his troops prior to invading the Transvaal.

The confluence of the Orange and Vaal Rivers in flood was an awe-inspiring sight, the forts etc. used in the siege of Mafeking brought back memories of the Relief of that town when boisterous crowds "Mafficked" in Glasgow, and when visiting the scenes of war, I was more than ever convinced that the old, white-haired gent was right when he protested that the war was engineered by British capitalists, and Jews.

On several occasions I visited Bulawayo, travelled regularly over the extensive System, on which I was proud to be connected with such a fine, efficient, and smart body of railway servants with whom it was a joy to be assisted.

My salary was £700 p.a. plus £250 p.a. plus 17/6d. per day relieving expenses, thus giving me an income equivalent to about £1280 p.a. Great was the thrill of receiving such appreciable advancement, but it was not equal to the joy I experienced when unexpectedly promoted from Clerk and Porter with a corduroy uniform to the position of Foreman with a smart blue-silver-braided uniform and 4/- per week increase in salary.

After getting the boys comfortably settled, Mum gave up house in Silver Street, Pretoria, and joined me in Kimberly during November, 1934, the year we attended the South African National Sunday School Association Convention in Bloemfontein, where we enjoyed the fellowship and the early Easter Sunday Morning Service on Signal Hill.

I linked up with the Sunday School, where I was a teacher, and Mum immediately joined the Women's Association, the ladies being anxious for her to become their President.

Life was happy in sociable, loveable Kimberly, with its terribly hot summers and freezing winters, but as elsewhere, railway and Sunday School occupied the most of my time, nevertheless I found time to take up bowling, even if I was half-hearted in regard to this form of sport.

Chapter 21
Pretoria

Two Months — 1935

The Rogans had struck their tent, and after only ten happy, all-too-short months, I was retransferred to Pretoria in the position of Superintendent (Commercial and Operating) at a salary of £1,000 p.a. It was a great honour to me, probably one of the finest compliments ever paid to a Union railwayman by the Management to be selected for such an important appointment on what had become my "Home" System, where I had been:

Trains Clerk,
District Inspector,
Acting Station Manager, Pretoria,
Senior Clerk, Rates, Claims, & General in System Office,
Chief Clerk to the Stores Superintendent,
Stores Superintendent, and now
Superintendent, Commercial & Operating.

I was humbly proud, acknowledging openly that my loving Heavenly Father had blessed me in my work and in our home, far beyond our expectations, and He gave me the grace, as he had done before in the Stores Department, to deal justly and considerately with all men, not excepting the Railway Institute stalwarts who had made things rather unpleasant for me in the days when I was the System Trains Clerk.

As at Kimberly and ever afterwards, a fully equipped bogie private saloon, with combined Lounge-Observation-Dining Room, two sleeping compartments, a full-size bath with hot and cold water, pantry, a large, fully equipped kitchen and accommodation for the native attendant, was placed at my disposal. The vehicle made travelling the essence of comfort and luxury.

Many changes were evident in the staff, both at Headquarters and on the System generally, improvements had been effected in track, stations, lines of communication, and signalling, a large number of new and heavier engines were working on the system, and many new industries had sprung into existence, including "Iscoor", since my departure from the Trains Office eight years previously.

I also had the use of a large railcar and a motor car, as required.

Travelling over the well-known and much-loved routes, I conversed freely with men of all grades, many of whom I knew when I was District Inspector.

All members of the staff were very friendly and cooperative, and when after two months of pleasant duty on the Eastern Transvaal System, I was offered a transfer, and I hesitated before accepting an appointment in Johannesburg — but I did.

During our altogether-too-short stay in Pretoria, Mum and I resided in a Private Hotel, Mack and Ian were residing in separate Boarding Houses, Harold was a student at Witwatersrand University, and Douglas was verry happy in Kimberly Boys High School, where he was a boarder in the school hostel.

We did not participate in church or Sunday School work, preferring to wait until we saw whether we were going to be settled in Pretoria, and as the transfer to Johannesburg came before we could make up our minds on the matter, we left without linking up again with any of the church's activities.

Actually, we were such a short period in Pretoria at this time that we had come and gone before most of our erstwhile friends and acquaintances realised the fact that we had been there at all.

John Andrew Rogan

Born 1911

Chapter 22
Johannesburg

1935-1937

Road Motor Manager

1937-1938

Superintendent-Operating (General Manager's Office)

I was appointed Road Motor Manager of the Union S.A.R. Road Motor Services, on the staff of the General Manager, Johannesburg at a salary of £1000 p.a., which was subsequently increased to £1200 p.a.

Completely divorced from railway work proper, I was given the sole use of a chauffeur-driven motor car and travelled extensively, on duty, through Zululand, Swaziland, Pondoland, Ciskei, Transkei, a portion of Basutoland, and throughout the whole of the Union from the North to the South and East to West.

The work of establishing the Motor Service had been thoroughly done, and I found it comparatively easy to continue on such a good foundation, and with the cooperation of a thoroughly efficient staff. The work was very interesting, but as with the Stores department, I had much to learn, and not the least part of my difficulties was to learn that I was not a railwayman, especially when travelling over systems where I had once been stationed.

During a car journey from Cape Town to Mossel Bay, I passed the place where the few passengers landed who were fortunate enough to reach shores from the ill-fated troopship S.S. Birkenhead, which struck a hidden rock and foundered in a matter of minutes.

We took up residence in Parkview, where Harold, who was at Wits University, resided with us and we joined Parkview St. Columba's Presbyterian Church, where my darling Mum became President of the Women's Association, and I continued my Eldership from St. Andrew's.

It had been the practice of the W.A. Ladies of St. Columba's Church to hold a yearly church bazaar on a large scale, but Mum, who knew that God answers prayer, decided in the face of much opposition to place the financial need of the church before God and to leave out the Bazaar. There was much shaking of heads, much pessimism, and needless opposition until the results of the day appointed for the final receiving of Freewill Offerings, when Mum's faith was greatly rewarded and the faithless were confounded by an amount exceeding the total receipts from any of the Bazaars ever held.

According to your faith be it unto you.
Matthew 9:29

Mr. Harold Edwin Rogan, M.A.

Born 1915

Killed 1944

1937-1938

Operating Superintendent, Johannesburg

If I was to become System Manager, my Heavenly Father must open another door through which I could pass to the very edge of System Managership, and in His won miraculous manner, He did so in quite an unexpected way, and I was appointed Senior Superintendent (now designated "Chief") Operating, on the staff of the General Manager for the Union Railways at a salary of £1200 p.a.

I was immediately under the Chief Traffic Manager, for whom I acted on several occasions when he was away from office.

It was a responsible position, requiring practically no travelling, but there was a large, thoroughly experienced administrative staff, who kept the wheels turning.

The work was within the scope of my wide experience, and I had no difficulty in arriving at important decisions in regard to the many and varied operating matters, which were placed before me from time to time.

We continued to be associated with St. Columba's Church, Parkview, without linking up with the Sunday School, and there was no other organisation of a spiritual nature, the Eldership only necessitating the formal delivery of the quarterly communion cards.

During 1937, Harold was awarded the Elsie Ballott Bursary, which enabled him to attend Cambridge University for three years (19371939) and six months at the Union College, New York. During his residence in England, he visited Holland, Norway, France, and Italy, not forgetting journeying through England and Scotland.

Our lovely family of boys were scattered, with Ian and Mack in Pretoria, Harold in England, and Douglas in Kimberly, but Mum and I were quite content to know that they were safe under His guidance and keeping, to whom they had all surrendered themselves in the days of their youth.

Time was slipping past quickly, I was approaching to within measurable sight of my pension, and my Heavenly Father knowing this was preparing the way for me to reach one of the topmost rungs in the Railway Service. The first step in the final stage came when I was instructed to proceed to Windhoek to relieve the System Manager for a period of six months.

Chapter 23
Windhoek

1938-1939

I left Johannesburg during October, 1938, for Windhoek, where I was required to relieve the System Manager, who had proceeded overseas for a period of six months leave, at a salary of £1200 p.a., plus £60 per annum, plus 17/0 per day continuous relieving expenses, or equivalent to approximately £1784 per annum. The victory was won to the glory of God, who as always had been true to his promise to do that which was right concerning me. True, I was not yet a permanent System Manager, but I never doubted but that the day would come when I would reach that much-coveted position as a permanency.

Crossing the Orange River at Upington recalled our first protracted journey when the low-level bridge was not visible under the flood waters, and Keetmanshoof appeared like an old friend with its spaciously built station and German environment.

I travelled over the whole system in my luxurious private saloon (No. 1 S.W.A. was still in use by the Assistant Superintendent) and made much use of my official motor car and the railcar, driven by a chauffeur and uniformed driver, respectively.

I occupied the spacious German-furnished office from where the German Director of Railways had issued instructions. Most of the staff were strangers to me, although a few of the 19231927 stalwarts were still in evidence.

The Namib Desert, with its sand and sand dunes, Walvis Bay, depressing and gloomy, Lüderitz, windswept on a rocky eminence, sand blasted

Kolmans Kop, and along the cultivated banks of the Orange River to Kakamas were not new to me, neither had they lost that allurement which South West Africa has for its admirers.

The Gobabis Line, which had been constructed during my absence in the Union, reminded me of the "Commercial Survey" trip during my previous residence in Windhoek, washaways continued to recur with monotonous, expensive, and disruptive regularity, and the Orange River in flood held me in its fascinating grasp.

Mum remained in Johannesburg until the end of February, 1939, and when she joined me during March, we resided in a hotel, and we planned to go overseas together immediately I was finished in Windhoek, but the "best-laid schemes o' Mice an' Men gang aft agley".

Chapter 24
Return to Pretoria

1939

Having been granted overseas leave, I reported back to Headquarters in Johannesburg, booked our passages, and the same day was requested to Relieve the System Manager for an indefinite period. Accordingly, I proceeded to Pretoria immediately, at the same remuneration minus £60 per annum that I had enjoyed in Windhoek, with the sole use of an official motor car, a railcar, and a fine, large private saloon, and Mum proceeded overseas by R.M.S. Warwick Castle.

I was thrilled beyond measure to return to the Eastern Transvaal System, especially for the third and last time, to occupy my eighth position, each one very different from the other on the same system, which I first reached from Port Elizabeth during 1917.

God had truly led me by devious paths to one of the most coveted positions on the Union Railways, and in all the years through sunshine and shadow, mixed with hopes and fears, our faith had not wavered or grown dim.

The majority of the staff congratulated me unsolicited, and their attitude was one of cooperation and friendliness, in all ranks from Station Masters to the humble shunter, white labourers, and a few of the old, faithful natives. I was among my own, and my own appreciated me.

One of the first incidents of my new position was the urgent dispatch of about 200 fully armed policemen to Windhoek, where the Germans awoke one morning to find machine guns looking menacingly at them from street corners. Hitler's thoroughly arranged plan to seize the Government of S.W.A. with hundreds of armed young Germans sent from Germany to German West Africa had been cleverly forestalled by General Smuts, who was Union Prime Minister at the time.

I travelled through the Kruger Park National Game Reserve and over the Magaliesberg Branch in company with the Railway Board, and with the Hon. Claude Sturrock, Minister of Railways on a motor car tour of inspection to Capital Park new works.

Everywhere there were signs of expansion in the industrial field of operation, I.S.C.O.R. works were increasing production, subsidiary industries were springing up in the western suburbs of Pretoria, new coal fields were being opened up, and new suburbs were in evidence in Pretoria, whilst on Nelspruit-Tzaneen-Rustenburg lines, the citrus and other developments were astounding.

After residing with me for some time in Windsor House Private Hotel, Mum proceeded overseas alone (see Chapter XXVIII), and we lifted our hearts to our Heavenly Father in praise and gratitude when she landed at Cape Town from the Cape Town Castle on the 31st of August, 1939.

World War No. II, as between Britain and Germany, was proclaimed on the 3rd of September, 1939, and South Africa declared war on the side of the Allies on the 6th of September, due entirely to the fearless political integrity and leadership of General Smuts, who gained a majority vote on the question of South Africa remaining neutral or otherwise, the chagrin of General Herzog and his much-disappointed Nationalist followers. The defeated Prime Minister retired to his farm and obscurity where he died a few years later.

The following article appeared in the "S.A. Covenant Message" for November, 1945, under the caption "Divine Intervention" throws Divine Light on how God does intervene, when necessary, in the Government of Nations:

Divine Intervention

How often during the global war some incident revealed how God overrules . . . at the beginning of the war an incident happened in South Africa which was to have a far-reaching result on the whole course of the war . . . An Allied leader expressed to Field Marshall Smuts the opinion that had S.A. gone wrong (i.e., not entered the war on the side of the Allies) the end might possibly have been different. . . .
General Hertzog had repeatedly promised he would summon Parliament before he decided on war, but he never undertook to consult Parliament should he decide not to go to war, and it had never struck anyone to ask him on the point . . . there is every reason to believe that he and his wing had decided to remain neutral.
. . . unique incidence saved S.A. from a dilemma . . . under the S.A. Constitution, all laws have to be passed by the House of Assembly and the Senate combined . . . law advisers discovered that the life of the Senate would expire in a few weeks, and unless both houses met to pass a law extending the period, no legislation passed by the Assembly alone would be valid.
. . . General Herzog reluctantly summoned Parliament for a brief three-day session in order to ensure this technical defect. The last thing he desired, or expected, was for war to burst upon him . . . this is precisely what happened . . . when Parliament met together he could not prevent the House taking a vote on the question "peace or war", and his plan . . . to remain neutral . . . was frustrated . . . the burden of his theme was S.A. should remain neutral. If Hitler won the war, he would not molest us, and if the British were victorious, we would be safe anyhow.

Parliament voted in favour of war by a small majority, and General Smuts became the man of the hour not only in S.A., but in all Allied countries, and Hitler's contemptuous remarks only showed more clearly Germany's disappointment.

Loyal South Africans were delighted, whilst the Republican-Nationalists expressed their chagrin in disparaging remarks and the more reckless by acts of sabotage and in other ways.

You men and women flocked in their thousands to the colours, Mack and Douglas were soon in uniform, by virtue of my position I was given the rank of Major in the Defence Force and threw my whole weight into the work organising the Transvaal Eastern System, ready for the great part it would have to undertake in maintaining the sinews of war by virtue of its strategical position, its coal fields, steel works, and many industries.

It was the fixed intention of the Railway Board to confirm me in the position of System Manager, Pretoria, (they told me so) but determined and successful opposition to my appointment on the part of several exNatal Officers who had gained the ear of the Minister of Railways resulted in an ex-Natal nominee being appointed, although he was my junior in the service.

The Railway Board, when expressing their regret to me, were very sore indeed that their recommendation had been set aside in favour of a junior and less-experienced officer, and I, without any feelings of resentment, thanks to God, prepared to lave immediately for Windhoek, S.W.A., to which system I had been appointed System Manager.

My Blessed Saviour had kept his promise, and but for His direct intervention on my behalf, I am of the opinion that I would never have reached the office of Superintendent, the jealousy, wordly antagonisms, and campaign of slander against me, having been such that humanely speaking, I could not have succeeded in reaching the top. But His peace, the peace which passeth all understanding, and which the world can neither give nor take away was vouchsafed unto me and Mum, enabling us to remain steadfast and unmoveable in the face of much opposition. The world abused, slandered, and crucified my Master and I could expect no less.

Chapter 25
Windhoek

1939-1941

For the third and last time, Mum and I travelled to Windhoek, where I had been appointed System Manager at a salary of £1400 p.a. plus £60 C.O.L with the sole use of an official chauffeur-driven motor car, a railcar, a private saloon, and the usual travel allowance.

From the time I had scrubbed floors at Maxwell Park on the Caledonian Railway, which was now merged with the L.M. and S. Railway, 41 happy, successful years had passed, and in less than two years I would be on pension. In the interval, I had been:

1898	Clerk and Porter	
1900	Station Foreman	
1902	Coaching Clerk	
1903	Goods Clerk	
1904	Operating Clerk — Rolling Stock	
	" " Accidents	
	" " Trains	
1910	Trains Clerk — Sr. Operating Clerk	
1910	" "	East London
1914	" "	Port Elizabeth
1917	" "	Pretoria
1923	Chief Clerk	Windhoek
1927	District Inspector,	Pretoria
1928	Acting Station Manager,	Pretoria
1929	Rates, General, & Claims, Sr. Clerk,	Pretoria
1932	Chief Clerk, Stores Department,	Pretoria

1933	Stores Superintendent, Stores Dept.,	Pretoria
1934	Superintendent, C and O,	Kimberly
1934	" "	Pretoria
1935	Road Motor Manager,	Johannesburg
1937	Superintendent (Sr.) Operating General Managers O.	
1938	System Manager (Relieving)	Windhoek
1939	System Manager (Relieving)	Pretoria
19391941	System Manager (appointed)	Windhoek

Windhoek, where we had spent happy years with our four beautiful boys, was changed, even since my relieving visit during 1938, and everywhere the Germans were truculent in their confidence that their day of emancipation from the yoke of detested "Mandate-ism" was near at hand. Hitler's victorious, highly mechanised army was smashing and slashing its way to victory without having suffered a reverse, and Britain was standing in her sea-bound isle, proudly defiant against overwhelming odds.

The civil servants were still strictly official, holding the railway at arms length, and even the comparatively highly paid System Manager of Railways (and his sweet wife) were not acceptable to the service — even down to the low-paid clerks.

I travelled the well-known system by rail in my private saloon, over atrocious roads far to the North and South by car, and on occasion proceeded by car to Walvis Bay to organise repairs required by the SS Ceramic, which had put into that port with an enormous rent in her side as the result of a collision in the South Atlantic.

My darling Mum and I took up residence in the System Manager's new, large house, which would have been more acceptable had we had our four boys with us.

During October, November, and December of 1940, we spent a holiday at Warner's Beach, where we received the news that our first darling grandchild (Allister) had been born, and East London, and on our return, we lived in a furnished house.

We were contented and happy finding our spiritual fellowship in each other's company and amongst a few faithful followers of the Lord outside church circles.

A large, new plant to condense seawater to fresh water had been erected at Lüderitz, the only one of its kind in the Southern Continent at that time, and I invited Dr. Conradie to undertake the opening of the new plant, which he very graciously consented to do.

Dr. and Mrs. Conradie, Administrator of S.W.A., Mr. & Mrs. D.D. Forsyth, Secretary for S.W.A. (Mr. Forsyth subsequently accompanied General Smuts to San Francisco and London), Mum and myself travelled by special train in private saloons to Lüderitz for the ceremony, a preponderatingly German town, where the population were glorying in the German victories, where we were liberally entertained with a public dinner, dances, and a trip to Pomona in the centre of the Consolidated Diamond Fields, where we extended our visit to Ellenboog, a peculiarly shaped rock on the rugged Atlantic coast south of Elizabeth Bay. The occasion was the church service conducted in Afrikaans which I arranged, attended by all of the visiting party and an overflowing congregation.

Father Time was overtaking me with rapid steps over a quickly decreasing space of time, and I travelled aimlessly, partly to keep out of the way at Headquarters, being anxious not to hinder the staff by my fast-disappearing presence. In this spirit, Mum and I visited Gobabis, on the fringe of the Kalahari Desert east of Windhoek, making use of my private saloon, and thus the sweet, you girl of 15 years who had asked me my name when I was dressed in a corduroy uniform accompanied me 43 years later in my saloon on my last official journey on the lines of the S.A.R. & H., at which time I was a System Manager.

It was not without a pang of regret that I handed over my Railway Pass, available over all African Railways south of the Equator, and walked out of my beautiful ex-German office, appropriately furnished with ex-German solid oak furniture, and thus parted with the railway after 43 years of faithful service.

I had enjoyed every moment of my service, first with the Caledonian Railway Company in Scotland, secondly with the Cape Government Railways in the Cape of Good Hope, and lastly with the South African Railways & Harbours, which in my considered opinion was the best organised and conducted of the three railways.

The S.A.R. & H., commencing with the amalgamation of the railways in the four provinces at Union, grew from what may be termed skeleton services to a gigantic organisation operating approximately 13,000 miles of railway, and at the time of my retirement, about an equivalent mileage of Road Motor Services.

The old, imported (of which I was one), and exImperial Army staff had practically disappeared, and in their places, there was a fine body of men, preponderatingly Afrikaans, of temperate habits, morally upright, of fine physique, enthusiastic, well-trained railwaymen.

Chapter 26
Valediction

There is an end to every road

1941

On the night of the 28th of March, 1941, the Railway Institute Hall, Windhoek, was filled to capacity with railwaymen, civil servants, police, and postal officials, together with their wives and members of the public. Dr and Mrs. Conradie, Administrator of the S.W.A., Mr. & Mrs. D.D. Forsyth, Secretary for S.W.A., the two Railway Medical Officers, and many other senior officials were in the representative gathering, assembled to wish Mum and I goodbye and God speed.

That afternoon I had relinquished the reins of office for the last time, and on the morrow I would be a "Railway Pensioner" without status and without a home, for the time being in a strangely different world of which I knew so very little after 43 years of zealous railway service during which long period I did not participate in sport, except for the year or two when I played bowls, my only interest being our happy home, church, and church activities.

The gathering was a happy one, laudatory speeches were made, Mum being mentioned in love and affection. Light refreshments were served, we were presented with two lovely oil paintings of S.W.A. landscapes and a portmanteau from the S.W.A. section of St. John's Ambulance Officers and members of which branch I was the District Commissioner.

Mum was presented with a handsome dressing-table set.

The road had been a long one, along which happiness flowed continually, and with my darling Mum ever ready to encourage and cheer, four beautiful, healthy boys in the house, and God in full control, it could not be otherwise.

We had been abundantly blessed, our cup of happiness was full to overflowing, and we stepped out into the future, mercifully all unknown, to live under entirely new conditions, sure in the knowledge that God was with us, whose goodness had never failed in all the years, praise be to His name.

I left the Roucan with the clothes I was wearing, 2/- in cash, arrived at Sterkstroom breakfastless with a similar amount of money out of my precious, jealously guarded £12. 0. 0., and at the close of my railway career, I could proclaim we have all and abound, our Loving Heavenly Father having supplied all our needs according to His riches in glory. Spiritually blessed, rich in our family, and sound in a material sense. Truly, God had been good, beyond all measure.

The Lochar Moss Road, with its heather-bordered sides, the call of the cuckoo floating sweetly through the air, and the lark ascending high in the early dewy morn, had led towards devious paths through great cities, over the ocean highway and High and Low velds, through dorp and town until the end of the Railway Road was reached in Windhoek, S.W.A.

> Does the road wind up-hill all the way?
> Yes, to the very end.
> Will the day's journey take the whole long day?
> From morn to night, my friend.

I had worked on 3 railways, under six General Managers of whom I conversed with four, eleven System Managers, and filled 22 different positions of widely differing character.

I had been a member of several different important committees, a member of the Johannesburg, Pretoria, and Windhoek Sick Fund boards, a member of the Railway Central Tender Board, a member of the District Inspectors Selection Committee out of whose report the large Railway Training College at Esselen Park has arisen, and where my photo may be seen in the Committee Group Photograph.

My life had been a full one, lived fearlessly in the presence of the Living God, of whose sustaining and ennobling power I was deeply conscious from the night I surrendered my life to Jesus in the Town Hall in East London.

One thing that stands out in my life more than anything else, more than life itself, is Mum's unwavering faith, courage, cheerfulness, and steadfastness in all our joys and sorrows, in our many transfers as well as in sunshine or shadow. Her life with its many good attributes and her steadfast love have meant more to me than all else put together, dating back to Maxwell Park (1898) and the days when I stole a glimpse of her, "My Angel", in the crowd of passenger streaming to and from the suburban trains.

I was in a new Heaven each time "My Angel" spoke to me, my every waking thought was of her, and the very fact that this sweet girl entered into my life kept me pure, and gave me victory and inspiration at the time when I most needed them.

Chapter 27
My Wife

All I have ever been, all I have and all I shall ever be, and I have already said God has blessed me in great measure, I owe to my darling wife without whose love, courage, faith in God and inspiration I would never have reached the high position of System Manager and neither would I have become the head of such a lovely home.

From Mum's arrival in South Africa "our home" her wonderful capacity for making lasting friendships, and her loving friendliness of spirit have been much appreciated by her wide circle of friends, and many tokens of love have been bestowed upon her.

It was an act of great, yet humble faith on her part when Peggy accepted a call to the Mission field as a worker in the St. Andrew's Colonial Homes, Kalimpong, India, when she sailed in November, 1904, and after five years fruitful service, during which time she won the hearts of workers and children alike, she sailed homewards during November, 1909.

I shared my darling's deep spiritual experience, and the pleasure I received from the knowledge that "my Angel" had gone to the Mission field completely obscured to my view the fact that we were irrevocably separated for 5 years, after not having seen each other for over two years. God had brought us together in loving unity, cemented by His Holy Spirit, and nothing on earth or heaven could separate us.

And Jacob served seven years for Rachel: and they seemed unto him but a few days for the loved he had to her.
Gen. 29:20

I told Peggy by letter of the glorious news of my conversion (1904) and from that time onwards our letters became more frequent, and more lovingly intimate until 1908, when we became engaged, when we became one in body, soul, and spirit. This was a great act of faith on our part, in view of our long separation, but we were unfaltering in our faith knowing that the Lord had brought us together for each other, and that the day of our marriage would come.

In Titwood Parish Church, Glasgow, there was a beautiful tablet (the church has since been demolished) with the name of the many workers, including Mum's name, who went from that Evangelical Centre to the Mission field in India, China and to other centres.

My Darling has been a beautiful, good, faithful wife and mother, always accepting our many transfers from town to town, and flitting from house to house, which were far too many but unavoidable, with cheerfulness, overcoming disappointments and discomforts with courage and resourcefulness where others would have failed. Her faithfulness in the cold spiritual atmosphere of the Presbyterian Church, eagerness to work in the Sunday Schools in the Railway Reserve, St. Paul's Church, Beach East London, and the Good Hope Mission, Pretoria, whilst supervising and maintaining our home, in a perfect state of efficiency were accomplishments which could only have been achieved by a practically minded woman wholly surrendered to the Lord Jesus Christ.

Mum is a generous giver of herself, in good works, and in kind, and wherever help is needed her large sympathetic heart pours itself out in overflowing love and when possible, practical assistance.

Whilst in India Mum gained a working knowledge of Hindustani, and at school she excelled in French.

When in Port Elizabeth my Darling was treated in the General Hospital for Renal Cholic, a most painful ailment, in Pretoria she was operated on for appendicitis and other complications, and later she had to visit the same hospital to have a refractory tooth removed. In Windhoek Pet spent a few days in hospital with a sore eye, and in Johannesburg the Lady Dudley Private Nursing Home was visited to have certain toenails removed. The General Hospital was also visited for a short period in connection with a duodenal ulcer, and later she was taken to the Libertas Nursing home, Johannesburg, seriously ill. Notwithstanding so many visits to hospitals, Pet was a healthy, happy, normal woman, loving and caring for her husband and children and was never happier than when engaged in her domestic duties.

In Pretoria Pet gained the Nursing certificate and the St. John's Ambulance Certificate, was awarded to her in Johannesburg, whilst a member of the C.P.S.

During the catastrophic war years (1939-1945) when the earth was shaken to its foundations, Mum's calm trustfulness, when calamity after calamity crashed in upon our home, was such that it cannot be expressed in words. Resignation and trust in God were Mum's sure defence, her refuge in the time of storm but for her source of spiritual power the clouds of grief which burst over Pet's soul like engulfing waves must surely have overwhelmed my precious Darling.

Four crushing blows:

> 1941 On the 24th of November, 1941, Douglas lost a foot in the battle of Sidi Resegh, near Sidi Omar, in the Libian Desert.
> 1942 Mack was wounded in the battle of El Amein, and although military classed him as "slightly injured" the bullet passed dangerously near to vital places in his skull.
> 1943 Mack was killed in an air crash near Irene, Transvaal, on the 9th of October, 1943.
> 1944 Harold was killed whilst on an operational flight in Italy on the 15th of April, 1944.

It is to be wondered at that we were all very anxious in regard to Mum's health and strength to ensure the terrible shock of the crushing news more especially as the sorrow of Mack's leaving us was still o'er flowing and Mum had just been discharged from Libertas Private Nursing Home, to where she was taken in a semi-conscious condition. But Mum's faith was wonderful to behold, and the Lord sustained her throughout the terrible years and gave her strength to carry on in the home.

Many daughters have done virtuously, but thou
excellest them all.
Prov. 31:29
My bellowed is mine.
S. of S. 2:16
Thou art beautiful Oh my love.
S. of S. 6:14

MY WIFE

My dear wee sweetheart darling, Pet
My own sweet precious love,
Though wandering far I love thee yet,
My Mummy, darling, dove.
What though the train moves slowly on,
Over the hills so steep,
I know there awaits me in our home,
My wife with love so deep.
The Southern Cross sinks in the sky,
The night is cold and clear,
My heart is light, my spirits high,
For Pet my love is near.
The wheels keep time with regular beat,
The mile posts slowly pass,
For every through is calm and sweet
I'm nearing home at last.
The lights ahead grow clear and bright
Work for the day is done,
I'm home at last, alight, alight,
Thank God for such a home.
How is my Pet, how are the boys,
Oh tell me all that's new,
It's grand to hear of all your joys,
It's grand to be with you.

Written in the train approaching Waterval Boven: 28 June, 1919. J.R.

OUR MUM

My dearest darling Mum,
With fair and lovelit face,
Who walks with such beautiful grace,
With neat and skilful hands.
What would we do without her,
Who is so kind and good,
Her pleasures with us to share,
She's always in good mood.

Windhoek,	Ian Rogan
S.W.A. 21.10.23	Aged 13

MY MOTHER

I ought to love my mother,
For there is not another,
Who has done so much for me,
With lovelit face, so full of grace,
With eyes so true, and deepest blue.

Windhoek,	Mackenzie S. Rogan.
S.W.A. 22.10.23.	Aged 10 1/2 .

Mr. J. Rogan

Taken when System Manager of Railways, Windhoek, S.W.A.

Mr. and Mrs. J. Rogan with private secretary and native coach attendant

Private Saloon No. 32

Taken at Gobabis, S.W.A. on the occasion of my last official journey

MY WIFE

Fine modelled brow and lovelit face,
Eyes, affectionate, soft and blue,
A voice so sweet, and form of grace,
A woman, noble and true.
Windhoek,   J.R.
S.W.A. 12.9.23

OUR MUM

Loving face and full of grace
I should love my mother,
I like her better than any other,
She always looks after us,
And yet we just make a fuss,
But now I am trying to be good,
Because she does everything.
She gets our clothes
And buys our food.
And when we are sick
She tries to get us well quick,
She does everything for us
And we just make a fuss,
But now I'm trying to help her
And I do love my mother
And my little brother too,
As a good boy would do.

Windhoek,   Harold Edwin Rogan
S.W.A. 23.10.23   Aged 8

The sun sets bathed in glorious hue,
And nature is at rest,
Our thoughts and prayers are all of you,
Our Dearest, sweetest, best.

Windhoek,   Dad
S.W.A. 1.12.23
Herein is love.   1 John IV-10

SWEETHEART

Her life is fragrant and ever sweet,
Our every thought inspires,
Now shall we live for this one week,
Without her zeal our life to fire.
Our Saviour, Lord, Thou friend of man,
Protect her night and day
Embrace her with Thy Heavenly arm
Keep her in Christ, The Way.
Oh, Jesus Lord, our Saviour Friend,
You know our sweetheart's trust
To her Thy protecting spirit send,
And bring her back to us.
Oh Lord our prayer is but threadbare,
Our faith in Thee is strong,
Watch o'er our Mum with special care,
And bring her back to home.
Dad

Written to Mum whilst she was attending a Presbyterian Women's Association Conference, concurrently with the Presbyterian General Assembly, in Kimberley, during 1929.

Mum Revisits Scotland

During the period I was relieving the System Manager, Pretoria, my Darling visited Scotland for the second time from South Africa, leaving Johannesburg in the Blue Train during June 1939, she voyaged in the R.M.S. Warwick Castle to Southampton, where Harold, who was then a student at Cambridge University, met her.

After a short stay at Bournemouth, London was visited and from there Mum travelled in the Coronation Scot to Glasgow where Mrs. Smith was residing alone, Mr. Smith having passed away on the 16th of April, 1935. Many old acquaintances were renewed, and happy memories recalled in the city which was so dear to us both. Harold, after a visit to Holland in connection with Youth Movement work, took Mum in his car to the beautiful Trossacks, and Pet visited the West Coast of Scotland, to as far north as Oban by Char-a-banc.

Mum and Harold then travelled by car to Dumfries, visiting the Roucan in passing, Wigtonshire, The Windermere Lakes, Keswick of Keswick Convention fame, Bolton, and Stratford on Avone where they visited the palatial theatre erected to perpetuate the memory of Shakespeare. It was an enjoyable, happy holiday, although the air was full of rumours of war in Britain and we all gave a sigh of relief when my Mum stepped off the Union Ltd. at Johannesburg after voyaging in the last trip of the R.M.S. Capetown Castle before the out-break of war, the vessel reaching Capetown on the 31st of August, 1939, and war broke out on the 3rd of September.

No other woman could have been to me, or guided my footsteps in the paths of righteousness and truth or been what my Darling has been to me during the years 1898 to the present day (1949) and to her sons she has been a wise, affectionate, loving mother, a guiding angel to whom they carried all their joys and sorrows, childish problems and worries in perfect confidence that they would be solved for them.

Without My Pet I would never have been able to climb the Railway ladder, step by step to the much coveted position of System Manager, and but for her steadfast faith in the Lord Jesus Christ, and unwavering courage, it is very problematical whether I could have kept at the same spiritual high level as that which I was able to maintain.

I was a very fortunate lad to meet such a precious jewel of a girl, a meeting which I am convinced was arranged in Heaven with effect from the most critical period in my life. A sweet, pure, beautiful girl, who became a woman among women, a devoted mother, adored by her family, a cheerful faithful companion and wife in joy and sorrow, whose whole life centres in and around her home and the crucified, Risen, Ascended Son of God.

Mum entered my life a few days after I joined the Caledonian Railway in Scotland, her sweet, inspiring influence has sustained me for over 50 years, and she accompanied me in my private saloon on my last official railway journey over the lines of the South African Railways and Harbours. Bless the Lord, Oh my soul, magnify His Holy name, and praise Him in all His ways.

Others have lived nobly and well, and my wife is among those precious souls who have lived nobly, uprightly, serving the Lord, and magnificently in all their ways.

Mr. and Mrs. J. Rogan

With children and grandchildren (1939?)

L to R. Front Row: Allister Rogan, Antoinette Rogan, Rodney Rogan, Mackie Rogan, John Rogan, Mrs. J.A. Rogan (Doris)

Back row: Mr. Douglas Rogan, Mrs. D.S. Rogan (Rosemary), Mrs. H.E. Rogan (Emmie), Mr. J. Rogan (Grandad), Mrs. J. Rogan (Grandma)

Foreground: Master John Rogan, Mrs. H.E. Rogan (Emmie), Miss Ivy Unsted

Front Row: Lieut. H.E. Rogan, Mr. J.A. Rogan, Allister Rogan, Mrs. J.A. Rogan (Doris), Miss Una Unsted.

Back Row: Grandpa and Grandma Rogan.

Chapter 28
On Pension

RAND DAILY MAIL, Saturday, 5th of April, 1941.

MR. J. ROGAN RETIRES.

S.W.A SYSTEM MANAGER.

Mr. John Rogan, M. Inst. T., System Manager of Railways, Windhoek retired from the Railway service on March 29th, after nearly 39 years Railway service. He joined the Caledonian Railway in Scotland, now incorporated in the L.M.S. early in 1898 and entered the service of the Cape Government Railways in 1902.

Mr. Rogan served at Sterkstroom, Molteno, Burghersdorp, East London, Port Elizabeth, Kimberley, Johannesburg, Pretoria, and Windhoek. At various times he filled the positions of Stores Superintendent, Road Motor Manager, in the General Manager's Office, Superintendent, Commercial and Operating, and relieved the System Manager in Pretoria.

He was a member of the Staff Training Committee, Chairman of the S.W.A. Sick Fund, and Housing Boards, and held the rank of Major (unattached) in the Active Citizens Force.

Mr. & Mrs. Rogan who have three sons in the Air Force intend settling in Johannesburg.

On the eve of his retirement from the service a social function was given by the Railwaymen of the South West Africa System, in honour of Mr. & Mrs. Rogan. Opportunity was taken of presenting them with two oil paintings depicting South West African scenery. A cheque was also handed to Mr. Rogan with the request that he purchase a writing desk or an easy chair, or some other useful article for himself, and Mrs. Rogan was given a leather dressing case and also a writing set. The St. John Ambulance Brigade presented Mr. Rogan with a leather suitcase.

On the 29th of March, 1941, Mum and I, who were very conscious of the nearness of God in our sense of loneliness looked wistfully back towards Windhoek as the passenger train, drawn by an obsolete S.A.R. engine, banked by an ex-German Railways engine, climbed, with many twinging and twistings through the Railway cuttings, towards Aris, where the Railway reaches a height of 5864 feet above sea level. In the hoarse-strained noise of the exhaust I could plainly hear the engine panting "I need more power. I need more power", whilst from the Banker at the rear of the train came a hollow-strained "Ek het die Krag. Ek gee die Krag", even the S.A.R. locomotives having qualified bi-lingually.

The coupling pin was withdrawn to disconnect the tanking engine on the summit with a sharp "yank", and the disconnecting of the vacuum pipe caused a longish, loudish "whizz" and we knew our last link with Windhoek had been severed for ever.

Cattle grazed peacefully alongside the line, snugly situated homesteads built during the German Regime nestled among the old knurled Kemeel-doorn trees which were growing on the sites where they stood, before the German occupation of S.W.A., the sun sunk gradually in a blaze of gorgeous hues, constantly changing colours, and all nature was at rest as we sat quietly in our compartment at perfect peace in our souls and with the world.

> Day is dying in the West,
> Heaven is touching earth with rest,
> Wait and worship while the night
> Sets her evening lamps alight
> Through all the day.
> Holy, holy, holy, Lord God of Hosts,
> Heaven and earth are full of Thee,
> Heaven and earth are full of Thee,
> Oh Lord most high.
> Day Is Dying in the West
> Unknown Hymnal

We passed through Rehoboth in the cool of the evening, Keetmanshoop, of washaway memories and where I saw General Hertzog on horseback, addressing a Commando of Hereros, was reached the following morning and at Upington a few Railway friends had gathered at the station to wish us Godspeed.

Crossing the new high-level bridge (the longest in the Union) over the Orange River at Upington we recalled our first adventurous journey northwards to Windhoek when the old Low-Level Bridge was not visible under the surging flood waters and our four wee boys were all excited at the thought of spending 3 nights in the train.

Breaking our journey at Kimberly we had the joy of meeting Mack and Douglas, who were in uniform stationed at Bloemfontein and Kimberley, respectively. Their manly bearing and obvious courage, which enabled them to do the right thing and join up in South Africa's hour of need, was a source of much joy and inspiration to us.

> Praise ye the Lord,
> Bless His holy name.

Our last Railway journey on Railway pass other than a holiday Pass, finished when we stepped from the train at Johannesburg where we were met and lovingly greeted by Doris and Ian, with whom we spent a short time in their lovely Greenside home.

After purchasing the dwelling house 30 Rutland Road, Parkwood, we proceeded to Durban where we remained until July, during which time I occupied the position of Hon. Treasurer (Assistant) to the Governor General's Fund.

We still reside at 30 Rutland Road, where these memoirs were written during 1949, and from where our manly, courageous boys of whom we are justly proud, left to give of their best in the North. We still see their parting wave, catch again the infection of their enthusiasm and long with an unsatiable yearning to hear the voices again of Mack and Harold of "rest awhile" until we meet again.

The world seems to be at rest, there is a stillness as the hush of evening, the Railway has almost faded out of our lives, the jealousies and juggling for position in the ranks of seniority, which I am proud to say never found a place in my busy life, have ceased to jar, and in our new found world we walk and talk with Jesus only. We can truly say,

I've found a friend in Jesus
He's everything to me.
If I've Jesus, Jesus only
Then my soul has found a gem.

May the glory of the Risen Lord,
Shine in me,
May the message of his holy word,
My inspiration be.
Durban, 1941   J.R.

With Christ I walk on lofty heights,
And clear pure air inhale
The Lord himself my guiding Light
His love shall never fail.
Windhoek, 1940.   J.R.

Looking back over the fast-receding years I am encouraged when I recall the many good friends and loyal co-workers, mostly Afrikaans speaking men (Dutch) of good education, upright in their bearing and disciples of the Lord in the truest sense of the word. My life has been enriched by my contact with them, and although we are now irrevocably separated it gives me great joy to know that many of the men holding responsible positions were my co-workers, even if they were much junior in the service.

Friends in the social world I could not make, with few exceptions, owing to my open aversion to playing cards, dancing, smoking, drinking, gambling and other social evils, but what I lost, in the eyes of the world, my Blessed Saviour made up to me in overflowing abundance and I recognise that He satisfieth the hungry soul and the he has filled my cup of satisfaction, in spiritual things, and joy to overflowing.

Oh soul of mine soar high
To God's eternal Son,
Inhale the pure, all sin decry
Let Christ His temple own.
1.12.31.   J.R.

Mr. and Mrs. J. Rogan

With children and grandchildren (1941?)

L to R Front row: Allister Rogan, Mackie Rogan, John Rogan, Antoinette Rogan

Back row: Mr. Douglas S. Rogan, Mrs. D.S. Rogan (Rosemary), Mrs. H.E. Rogan (Emmie), Grandad and Grandma Rogan, Rodney Rogan, and Mr. J.A. Rogan

L to R. Antoinette Rogan, Grandma Rogan, Mrs. J.A. Rogan (Doris). Mrs. D.S. Rogan (Rosemary). Mrs. H.E. Rogan (Emmie)

Chapter 29
Family Life

God setteth the solitary in families.

Ours was a happy family in every sense of the word, our four sturdy boys, who loved their home, Sunday School, Church, Day School, Scouts, and Sport, grew up from childhood to manhood as plants beside an ever-flowing stream. With love and motherly wisdom Mum to whom they went with all their problems, guided them wisely in all their affairs.

From early years the boys were taught to love Jesus, and in youth, as well as in manhood, they continued to love and serve him with pure hearts.

Many were their quaint childish expressions, one incident which stands out in my memory was the occasion on which Ian, when quite a young chap, asked me if God drowned the fish in the flood, and Mack followed with the remark that "God must have had a hard job to drown the ducks."

Ian and Mack were students at Dale College, Kingwilliamstown, for two years, residing in the Presbyterian Hostel for boys, the other schools attended by them being Miss Duncan's Kindergarten (Ian in Port Elizabeth), Sunnyside, Pretoria, Secondary School, Windhoek, S.W.A., Public School and the Pretoria Boys High School.

Harold, the most scholarly in our family, took a 1st class Matriculation in the Boys High School, Pretoria in the year 1932, when he was awarded the much-coveted old boys prize, awarded to the best scholar of the year, a good sport and who was popular with teachers and boys alike. He proceeded to Wits University in 1933 and graduated with a B.A. degree in 1935, with honours in two subjects.

During 1936 Harold attended the Johannesburg Normal College where he gained his Transvaal Teachers Certification at the end of the year, at the same time carrying off every prize it was possible for him to gain.

Having been awarded the Elsie Ballott Bursary (£400 p.a. for 3 years) Harold proceeded to Cambridge University in 1936 and graduated with his B.A. degree (Cantab) during 1937. Continuing his studies in Theology at Christ Church and Westminster, Cambridge, gaining distinction in Psychology which is not usual. After completing his studies our boy proceeded to Union Theological Seminary, New York, U.S.A. to finish off his education and when in the States he travelled down the Eastern seaboard as far as the Mexican border, returning through the Middle West. Whilst at Cambridge Harold visited Holland, Norway, France, Italy, and a small portion of Austria.

Douglas was educated at Windhoek, S.W.A., Sunnyside, Pretoria, the Boys High School, Pretoria and Kimberley B.H.S., where he resided in one of the hostels, and took his matriculation during 1037.

All the boys were keen scouts, but Mack, Harold and Douglas were particularly so, enjoying the scout camps and Mack and Harold accompanied a part of scouts to the Victoria Falls, Zimbabwe Ruins, The Matopos, and other places of interest.

Lieutenant Mackenzie Stewart Rogan

Left: Aged 30   Right: New Cemetery, Roberts Heights

Probably more than anything else Mum and I had great joy in the knowledge that our four boys knew and loved Jesus, and our evening Bible reading and Prayer circle, Sunday School, and church were as eagerly anticipated by them as they were by us.

They grew in beauty side by side.
They filled on home with glee.
The Graves of a Household
Felicia Hemans (1825)

	Born	Date
John Andrew (Ian) Rogan	East London	26.8.1911
Mackenzie Stewart (Mack) Rogan	East London	20.1.1913
Harold Edwin Rogan	Port Elizabeth	30.9.1915
Douglas Smith Rogan	Pretoria	25.10.1919

Our three beautiful daughters-in-law:

	Born	Date
Annie Doris Wylie	East London	22.5.1913
Emmie Unsted	Benoni	4.5.1914
Rosemary Middleton	Johannesburg	16.10.1922

ROLL OF HONOUR

LIET. MACKENZIE STEWART ROGAN, SAAF, CRASHED ON RIETFONTEIN FARM, near IRENE, TRANSVAAAL. 9.10.1943

Mack was wounded in the battle of El Alamein on the 23rd of October, 1942, when a bullet grazed his skull. He was sent to Tel Aviv to recuperate and after refusing home leave he returned direct to his squadron (24th) with which he remained until the cessation of hostilities in North Africa, after which he proceeded to the Union on leave.

On completion of his leave Mack was posted to Darling, Saldana Bay, Cape Province where he was engaged on the South Atlantic patrol work and in shepherding convoys into Table Bay. Subsequently he was sent to West African Port (probably Lagos) being one of the crew required to navigate a "Ventura" to the Union and when within two minutes (flying time) of Waterkloof Drome the plane crashed, when the crew of 3 were killed.

PRESS CUTTING.

RAND DAILY MAIL.

Lieut. Mackenzie Stewart Rogan, S.A.A.F. aged 30, who was killed in an air crash near Pretoria on Oct 9, was the second son of Mr. & Mrs. J. Rogan, 30 Rutland Road, Johannesburg and brother of the famous one-legged South African Pilot, Lieut. D.S. Rogan D.S.O. He returned recently from the Middle East where he served 16 months with a bomber Squadron, and was continuously in action. In the opening phase of the battle of Alamein Lt. Rogan was wounded, but later re-joined his squadron and operated until the closing stages of the North African Campaign.

Lieutenant Harold Edwin Rogan

Aged 28

Foggia Cemetery, Where First Interment Took Place

Mack is buried in the new Military Cemetery, Roberts Heights, around the spot where the plane crashed at Rietfontein there is an iron railing with the names of the killed on a plate affixed to the gate, his name is on the Roll of Honour plaque in St. Andrews Church, Pretoria, in Wits University, Johannesburg, in Dale College, Kingwilliamstown, where a framed photo of him in his uniform has been hung and on the Scout War Memorial at Gilwell, Florida.

LIEUT. HAROLD EDWIN ROGAN, S.A.A.F., seconded to R.A.F., CRASHED NEAR FOGGIA, ITALY. 15.4.1944

Harold joined the S.A.A.F. during January, 1941, being posted to the Aptitude School (or College) but not content with sending others on dangerous expeditions, he longed to be with them, and at his earnest request he was allowed to take "Wings" and in doing so was awarded the silver shield having taken first place in his course.

After gaining experience in the manipulation of the large four engine plane – the Liberator – he was posted to a drome near Foggia, Italy where he was continually engaged on more than ordinarily dangerous operations.

A telegram was delivered to 30 Rutland Road:

Department of Defence deeply regrets to inform you
that cable advice just received stated that 209297V
Lieut. Harold Edwin Rogan was killed 2357 hours
14 April. Air craft crashed on take off one kilometre
east of San Marco, near Foggia, Italy, Dewarec.

What had happened, had there been an earthquake or some great
catastrophe happening; why was the glory of the sun dimmed, why all these
callers at our home and the constant ringing of the telephone, followed
by sheaves of letters and many telegrams. It could not be true, but . . .
there was the telegram, the press notices . . .. And the condolences and so
gradually our dulled, stupefied, and numbed thinking began to awaken
to the fact that Harold would not return home when the boys came back
and that somewhere in Italy he was numbered with the honoured dead.

Harold's life was a fragrant one, his smile winsome his clear blue eyes
re-assuring and kindly, and he was greatly loved by everyone, and adored
by many.

His name is on the Roll of Honour in:

Pretoria Boys' High School
Wits University
Cambridge University
St. Andrew Presbyterian Church, Pretoria, and on

A communion table in St. Stephens Church, Rosettenville,
Johannesburg, with a silver, inscribed plate thereon, commemorates the
fact that Harold was an elder of that church, a marble tablet on the wall of
the entrance "Cross" at Roberts Heights new cemetery links him with his
brother Mack who is buried there, whilst he lies far from those who loved
and esteemed him so dearly in Bari Military Cemetery, Italy.

A letter written by Harold before his death, which indicates his loving thoughtfulness for his parents.

Lt. H.E.Rogan, 209397V

6 Dec. 43

My Dear Mum and Dad,

I'm writing this at the beginning of what may be a dangerous stage in my training. If you get it, it will mean that you have suffered yet another blow through this war. I want to try to soften that blow slightly if I can. You will feel sad and disappointed that after all the care and love you have put into my upbringing, and all the promise I have shown, my life has been cut off before I had a chance to achieve anything. But I think we should avoid looking too much to achievement as a test of successful living. Let's rather take life day by day. A picture is not to be judged by its size, nor a life by its length. I have lived happily. I have seen the world, I have enjoyed learning, I have made friends and known the joys of a home. If my life is shortened by a few years, what is that against the background of the ages. If my ambitions for the future have been trampled on, I know that really my contribution to the progress of humanity would have been just a drop in the ocean.

I wish I could have spared you this and I could have, if I have been satisfied with a soft job. But I think you'll understand that I had to make the decision to take up flying. I couldn't remain in a soft job – especially since I felt that it was not a vital war job in spite of all the publicity its been given – as long as my friends and brothers were suffering in the field. I have often been haunted by the thought of Ronnie Watson and lots of other in P.S.W. camps. I could be happy in Littleton.

Thank you for all you have done for me. I couldn't have wished for a better home. The thought of Mack's and Douglas' courage has often kept me going. Its only since I came up here that I have realised that their courage really is something exceptional. You have reason to be proud of them. I'm not much in the courage line myself, but I'm doing my best.

You will feel sad, but don't feel hopeless. I would have liked to live my life out, but since that is not to be I'll go on to the next step with a strong hope, and we'll meet again.

Lots of love always.

Harold.

Monthly record of St. Andrew's Church, Pretoria, May, 1944:

The news of the death of Lieut. Harold Rogan came as a great shock to us all. . . . Harold preached in St. Andrews, and we remember the quiet manner and deep conviction of his heart.

Six months ago, his brother Mackenzie was killed in an air crash just south of Pretoria. . . .

Lieut. Rogan joined the psychological testing unit and from there transferred to the air Force, qualifying as a pilot. He was killed in an air crash over Italy. His lovable personality, his clear brain and his strong spiritual, moral, and social convictions are a great loss to us. . . .

St. Stephen's Presbyterian Church, October 20th, 1944:

The memorial sacred to the memory of "Harold Edwin Rogan", took the form of a Communion Table in Gothic panelling, was made of Burmese Teak, and is a beautiful piece of work. A silver plate denotes it.

Pretoria Boys' High School (War Memorial Fund)

6.9.47

. . . I personally have proud memories of your two boys, both of whom it was my privilege and pleasure to teach here. They were fine lads, of high moral courage and a deep and sincere appreciation of duty.

. . .

St. Stephen's Presbyterian Church, Johannesburg

Sunday evening, May 21, 1944:

A service in loving remembrance of Harold Edwin
Rogan, R.A.F., who was killed on active service in
Italy, April 14th, 1944.

Epitome of sermon preached by the Rev. W.M. Kinsey, C.F.

These all died in faith. . . . Heb. XI. 1316.
. . .so in the midst of sorrow we find glory, this glory
that those we love . . . have been true to the highest
instincts man has learned from God, and learned
from God in Christ on Calvary.
Among such is our friend, Harold Edwin Rogan. He
began life with a rich family heritage of Christian
culture. He was unusually endowed with a clear logical
mind coupled with a soul enriched by personal faith
and deep consecration. His school career was a steady
climb in both study and personal enrichment. . . . he
took a First Class Matriculation. . . . and with it the
first for the most popular student (F.B.H.S.). At Wits
he took his B.A., and at the Normal College when
studying for his teacher's certificate took the Elzie
Ballott Scholarship which sent him to Cambridge. .
.at Cambridge he again took his B.A. with distinction
in psychology. . .he loved youth. . . . meantime he
did preaching work of a clear definite kind. He found
fellowship in the Oxford Group and made abiding
friends.
Whilst teaching at Sir John Adamson's School he felt
the pull of the war. He won his "Wings" and the silver
shield. He passed through the cubs, the scouts, and
the rovers.

His active brain, lit by a soul inspired by the spirit of
Christ found amazing opportunities for new service
and new knowledge. . . . he found time to undertake
study for the Diploma in Bantu Administration and
life. He was learning Sesuto. . . . he corresponded
across the world with Great Britain, the U.S.A., and
the West Coast of Africa with European and Native
friends.

He was an ordained Elder of St. Stephen's church,
but his whole life was a ministry. . . .

NEW LEADERSHIP

A CHRISTIAN FORUM FOR YOUTH

A MODERN HERO

In memoriam of

HAROLD EDWIN ROGAN

Killed in Italy, April 14th, 1944

(condensed)

On a spring day in Italy. . . . his comrades laid to rest a very gallant
gentleman. Harold Rogan, killed with his crew as they were taking off
in a Liberator plane for an enemy target. . . . he had a deep faith rooted
in a much clearer vision of Christianity than most people possess. South
Africa can ill spare men of Harold's gifts. . . . his unostentatious but deep
scholarship. . . . his love of the boys and girls. . .his quiet humour. . . .
his eyes, so merry, so unafraid, so straight always and his unflinching,
unwavering sense of what was right, backed by his courage to carry it out.

. . . Lovable and of rare ability . . . a leader who inspired . . . awarded
a special scout prize in the Annual Pretoria District Patrol competition for
his "wonderful way of handling his boys." People in all part of the world
are proud to count hi as a friend. Pretoria B.H.S. won the prize for most
popular student in the year that he took his Frist Class Matric. At the
University of the Witwatersrand, he took a double first in his B.A. degree,
in the year that he was Chairman of the S.C.A. following this winning the
Elsie Ballot Scholarship to Cambridge, while studying for this Teacher's

Certificate. At Cambridge he took his B.A. with distinction in Psychology, returning after his six months study at the Union Theological College, New York, to teach in Johannesburg. He joined the Aptitude Section of the Air Force and for one who loved peace and beauty, sincerity, and gentleness as he did it was difficult to decide to transfer to flying. He took first place in his course. His career was immeasurably enriched by his character of rare nobility. His achievements were the expression of the energy of a keen mind. We remember him in athletics, gentle teasing, advice diffidently given, when asked for, his fearless declaration of his beliefs.

On the Cape Beach he spoke to a group of children on the "whole armour of God." Few would find that armour as well fitting as it was to Harold. Harold is one with Bunyan's Pilgrim:

> Who would true valour see
> Let him come hither
> One here will constant be
> Come mind, come weather
> There's no discouragement,
> Shall make him once relent
> His first avowed intent
> To be a pilgrim.

Let us grieve, not for him, but for ourselves that we are so unworthy of the sacrifice of men like him. We can make that better world for which they fight and die a reality in our sphere at least. Shall we try?

Dora Mabin,

Johannesburg

THE STAR

Johannesburg

Saturday, 20th of May, 1944

Lieut. H. E. Rogan, S.A.A.F., aged 28 third son of Mr. & Mrs. John Rogan of Parkwood, Johannesburg, has been killed in Active Service, while flying with a Liberator Squadron in Italy. He leaves a widow and a son aged 3.

One of his brothers, Lieut. M.S. Rogan, was killed in an air crash near Pretoria last October. Another brother, Captain D.S. Rogan, D.S.O. lost a leg in air combat but returned to operations with an artificial limb.

UNIVERISTY OF WITSWATERSRAND

JOHANNESBURG

ROLL OF HONOUR

Members of the University who lost their lives on Active Service.

STUDENTS

Mackenzie Stewart Rogan

GRADUATES

Harold Edwin Rogan

PRETORIA BOYS' HIGH SCHOOL

The School Roll of Honour

Harold Edwin Rogan

Mackenzie Stewart Rogan

BUCKINGHAM PALACE

The Queen and I offer you our heartfelt sympathy in your great sorrow.

We pray that your country's gratitude for a life so nobly given in its service may bring you some measure of consolation.

GEORGE R.I.

Mrs. & Mrs. J. Rogan

30 Rutland Road,

Parkwood, Johannesburg.

Union Defence Force.

To Mrs. J. Rogan.

The Union Government in handing you the enclosed plaque of Remembrance and Replica in the form of a Brooch does so in grateful remembrance of the supreme sacrifice made by your son Lieut. M.S. Rogan.

Now that the war has been won and victory achieved it is hoped that this small token of appreciation by a grateful country, may comfort you a little in the days to come and that you will be the prouder for knowing the sacrifice was no in vain.

May I be permitted to express my personal sympathy in your bereavement.

J. SMUTS

Minister of Defence

"The Star", 20th of May, 1944

THE ROGAN'S SACRIFICE

For the third time yesterday the human tool of war brought its message to the Parkwood home of Mr. & Mrs. John Rogan. The first time, in 1941, their youngest son (now Captain Douglas Smith Rogan, D.S.O) had his leg shot off in action in Sidi Rezegh. In October last Mackenzie Stewart

Rogan was killed in an air crash near Pretoria. Yesterday they learned that Lieut. Harold Edwin Rogan, aged 28 had been killed in Italy on active service with a Liberator Squadron.

BRILLIANT SCHOLAR

Of the flying Rogans Harold was perhaps the most gifted.

. . . he took a 1ˢᵗ-class matric at the B.H.S., Pretoria, his B.A., at Wits., and whilst studying for his teacher's certificate, he was awarded the Elsie Ballott Scholarship at Cambridge.

. . . Thy brother shall rise again.
. . . I know that he shall rise again in the Resurrection of the last day.
. . . I am the resurrection and the life, he that believeth in me, though he were dead, yet shall he live.
St. John 11:2325

THE TRANSVAAL EDUCATIONAL NEWS.

MAY, 1944

H. E. ROGAN.

A Tribute.

The death on active service in Italy of Lieut. H. E. Rogan, came as a sad blow to his friends in Johannesburg, and especially to his colleagues on the staff of Sir John Adamson's J. H. School. All who came in contact with him knew with pleasure and joy his unostentatious but deep scholarship, his love of the boys and girls, among whom he worked, and perhaps best of all his quiet humour. But perhaps only those who knew him most intimately realised his utter loathing of the ways of war and his devotion to the arts of peace: his sacrifice was truly along the hard path of duty.

Oh our Sons, Mack and Harold, our Sons, our
Sons, would God I had died for Thee, Oh Mack
and Harold, our Sons, our Sons.
[Adapted from] 2 Sam. 18:33
In Thy presence is fulness of joy.
Psa. 16:11

THE MINSTREL BOY

The Minstrel Boy to the war is gone,
In the ranks of death you'll find him;
His father's sword he hath girded on,
And his wild harp slung behind him;
"Land of Song!" said the warrior bard,
"Though all the world betray thee,
One sword, at least, thy rights shall guard,
One faithful harp shall praise thee!"
The Minstrel fell! But the foeman's chain
Could not bring his proud soul under;
The harp he loved ne'er spoke again,
For he tore its chords asunder;
And said "No chains shall sully thee,
Thou soul of love and bravery!
Thy songs were made for the pure and free,
They shall never sound in slavery!"
Thomas Moore

Lieut. Mackenzie S. Rogan, S.A.A.F., killed in air crash, near Irene, Transvaal. 10th of October, 1943.

Lieut. Harold Edwin Rogan, S.A.A.F., seconded to R.A.F., killed on operational flight, Italy, 15th of April, 1944.

In peaceful scenes they rest awhile,
'Midst the glorious dead.
They live again in better land
Christ called them on ahead.
They'll rise again from earth's cold grave,
We know that this is true,
From out the sky they will appear
And Christ is coming too.

We'll meet again in heaven above,
We have a blessed tryst,
We'll speak to them and walk with them,
And praise the risen Christ.
We'll watch and pray and wait the day
To join them on that shore
Midst heavenly scenes in endless joy
To live for evermore.

They are in Christ, God' only son
Enjoying life anew,
We see their face and fragrant lives
In flowers of every hue,
In friendly voice and song of bird
We hear their loving tone
By faith we know we'll meet again
In our Eternal home.

J.R.
Johannesburg,
July, 1945.

Lieut. C. Nethersole, Pilot S.A.A.F.

Lieut. Mackenzie S. Rogan. Wireless Operator and Gunner. S.A.A.F.

Air Mechanic Stile, S.A.A.F.,

Killed in air crash east of Irene, 9 October, 1943, whilst navigating a "Ventura" Plane to the Union.

Outstretched wings 'gainst a sky of blue,
Cleaving the clouds, o'er mountain peak,
Down Africa's vast expanse they flew
In happy mood they vigil keep.
On horizon clear, their landing drome,
Their tank well done, now journey's end,
They crash, cruel fat, in sight of home,
Oh god, we ill could spare such gallant men.
They peacefully rest in soldiers' grave
In hallowed spot for ever dear,
They gave their all, and with the brave,
They live again in higher sphere.
Upright and true their all they have,
A coward's fears they did not know
Dauntless and strong, with spirit brave,
Knowing themselves, they feared no foe.
They danger knew in war zone flights
Unclouded was their view of heaven,
They live anew in loftier heights,
In vain they have not striven.
J.R.
Johannesburg,
19.11.43

Lieut. Harold E. Rogan, killed on operational flight with R.A.F. in Italy, 15.4.1944.

Beloved of all, loving, kind
In Christ The Way he trod,
With vision clear and noble mind,
Trusting the One True God.
The parting came, the dreaded hour,
We tried to laugh, encourage, cheer,
Looking to him whose risen power
Allayed our hidden fear.
Long pathless ways in giant plane
On perilous flight 'neath Northern sky
Where snow capped peaks in silence reign
He served with courage high.
O'er turbulent sea and flak strewn zone,
In freedom's cause he dared,
On journeys far with deadly bomb
The risks of war he shared.
He sleeps our husband, father, son,
'neath shady trees with comrades brave,
His warfare o'er, his work well done,
He lives beyond the grave.
J.R.
Johannesburg.
July, 1945

LIEUT. HAROLD E. ROGAN

Into the dark and pathless sky
He sped on wartime flight,
Nor dreamed that giant mountain tall
Was lurking in the night.
Deep sonorous sound disturbed night's peace,
And echoed round the peak,
His spirit fled from earthly home,
The Risen Lord to greet.
Midst massive rock on mountain steep,
The earth enwrapped in cloud,
Where eagle perch on perilous shelf,
Sky warriors brave and proud,
The twinkling stars saw tragic scene,
Above the haunts of men,
He lifeless lay, 'neath misty cloud,
In silence of the Ben.
From dark crevice deep the Connies crept,
Their idle day begun,
And twixt the crags his body lay
Caressed by morning sun.
His hair bejewelled with mountain dew,
Fanned in the morning breeze,
And eyes that saw a heavenly light,
Beyond the stately trees.
With hope adrift in surging fear,
Men skanned the morning sky,
And o'er the scene 'neath mountain haze,
The angels hovered nigh,
A gentle zepher fanned his brow
And tossed his wavy hair,
In sky above with deadly load,
Planes cleaved the chilly air.
Behind the Alps the sun sank low,
Framed in flaming gold,
Night's mantle fell across the scene
A dewy covering cold.
The early sun burst through the cloud,
And kissed his pallid cheek,
They found him there, 'midst boulders great

204 | John Rogan

'Neath the mountain peak.
With honours full they buried him,
A cross denotes his grave,
And strong men wept it in silence
In presence of the brave.
He gave himself for freedom's cause
And counted not the cost,
He lives again in Christ the Lord
With saints a mighty host.
J.R.
Johannesburg.
27.4.1947.
Jesus Christ . . . the first begotten of the dead, and the
Prince of the Kings of the earth. Unto Him that loved
us, and washed us from our sins, in His own blood.
Rev. 2:5

Captain Douglas Smith Rogan, D.S.O.

S.A.A.F., 1943

LIEUT DOUGLAS SMITH ROGAN, 103447, A.H.2, S.A.A.F., U.D.F., M.E.F., A.P.O., DURBAN.

Douglas who was a member of the Defence Force went into camp at Sonderwater with the Transvaal Scottish, for Active Service Training, on the 21st of May, 1940, transferred to the S.A.A.F. as a pupil pilot during July, 1940, and after taking his "Wings" left for the North during July 1941.

In the battle of Sidi Rezegh, one of the fiercest battles fought in North Africa, Douglas, whilst ground strafing lost a foot on the 24th of November, 1941, and after spending seven months in hospital he returned to the Union during May, 1942, his fine stamina and courage, aided by good nursing having enabled him to survive the terrible ordeal.

After having been fitted with an artificial leg, and permitted to demonstrate that he had lost none of his prowess and dash in handling a plane in the air, he returned to the North for the second time and re-joined his squadron at Daba.

During his second period of service in the war zone, Douglas was awarded the D.S.O. for conspicuous bravery and fought with his squadron until August, 1943, witnessing the surrender of the Italians and Germans in North Africa, operated over Panteleria Island, from Hengela Landing strip, North Africa, near Cape Bon, was stationed for a short period in much bombed and contested Malta, where his daily ration consisted of a few tabloids which did not satisfy the hungry gnawings but they did keep body and soul together.

When the troops landed in Sicily from North Africa, Douglas operated with the planes forming an umbrella and saw the unforgettable sight of some 2000 ships, many of them firing guns on to the mainland, approaching the shores of that Island, and was subsequently one of the first four pilots to land in Sicily.

Returning to the Union to undergo another severe and painful operation during August, 1943, Douglas when discharged from hospital was posted to Waterkloof Air Station, having in the meantime been promoted to the rank of Captain, and he finally took his discharge during December, 1944, after 5 years of courageous sacrificial service of which the military authorities were not unmindful.

RAND DAILY MAIL, 16.8.43

South Africa's one-legged pilot, Lieut. D.S. ("Shorty") Rogan, who has been awarded the Distinguished Service Order, is with an operational squadron in Tunisia. . . . He had his leg shattered by an explosive bullet from the machine gun of a German Tank when he was engaged in ground strafing at Sidi-Omar in 1941. . . . He is only the third Pilot on record – the R.A.F. ace, Bader, being the first – to go into action with an artificial limb.

Captain Douglas Rogan

D.S.O., S.A.A.F., Aged 24

EXTRACTS from BEYOND THE LAAGER

By Louis Duffus

(Chapter V of the book is devoted entirely to Douglas)

The Rogan Brothers became imbued, as good scouts should, with the Scouts high ideals of service.

By long distance observers of the war few men were accorded a higher place in the sanctity of the brave than those who went into battle with. . . . one leg, as if their disability became a personal challenge to manhood that spurred them to perform abnormal feats of gallantry and endurance. . . .

. . . Douglas Smith Rogan, a 22-year-old articled clerk. . . . an anti-aircraft shell all but severed his right leg below the knee but within a year he was back on operations with an artificial leg, shooting down more of the enemy. . . .

It was at Sidi Rezegh when the Union's army lost its 5th Brigade. . . . No. 2 Squadron went out at ten o'clock in the morning. . . . returned without loss and at 3-3:30 p.m. when the Squadron when out again . . . it was Rogan's 20th Operational sorties. . . . they flew low. . . . Rogan was hit in the right wing, and swerved to avoid the heavy concentration of fire when there was a crash in the cockpit and the oil filter was shattered. . . . billows of black smoke poured from the engine. . . . Rogan knew he had been hit in the right leg for it just fell off the rudder pedal, and he could not lift it back again. There were other wounds in the right hand and left thigh and blood flowed in the boot. With one leg useless, an arm pressed to his side, and two other wounds, he returned to the urgent task of landing the plane. . . . he took the water bottle and poured water over his head. . . . and down his throat and it restored waning strength . . . for over 40 minutes, weak and bleeding, he flew doggedly on and down he came to make a normal landing. . . . The next thing he knew was lying under the wing with an R.A.F. Medical Officer bending over him . . . Medical Officers were holding a conference about his shattered leg, and by this time I knew my leg was off. . . . the thought of losing a leg did not worry me as much as having to give up. . . . Rogan thought continually of Bader and set his heart on returning to action within a year. . . . By October, 1942, he was back in the Middle East. . . . he was in action with No. 1 Squadron flying spitfires and covering the break through at El Alamein. . . . His second tour embraced the advance to Tunisia via Malta to Sicily. . .he shot down to enemy planes. . . .scored two probables, and damaged one. . . . His was the fourth D.S.O. to be won by an Airman of the S.A.A.F. . . . the citation said ". . . for remarkable determination, courage and devotion to duty of the highest order." . . . His Spitfire was badly shot up over Marble Arch. . . . he was uninjured, but a bullet had neatly opened his tin of sardines. . . . he flew the plane from Agedabia [Ajdabiya] to the repair base where he spent the night with his brother Flight Sergeant (subsequently Lieut.) Mackenzie Stewart Rogan, S.A.A.F. at Tzimi.

EXTRACT from Twenty Angels Over Rome

By Richard McMillan

We were talking about the second front and the heroism it would call forth. . . . so I told the story of the lads. . . . the Spitfire pilots. . . a story that made my heart stir with pride. . . . it is the story of a youth who was a hero to everyone, except himself. The pilot a boy of 22 scrambled out and I recognised him . . . Douglas Rogan . . . a South African Scot serving with the R.A.F. . . . I noticed something new . . . the D.S.O. . . . Douglas was not the talkative type. . . . the battle of Sidi Rezegh roared at full height. . . . Douglas was flying a Kittyhawk. . . . an ack-ack shell got him . . . in the right leg . . . severed it . . . they were all heroes on that field, their courage beyond question. But for Douglas, his heroism was a fact he never acknowledged for himself. . . . I remember him well, his spirit forever marked by cheerfulness and indefatigable determination, no matter the odds he faced. . . . Yes, I think in trying to define courage Doug's story fills the bills. . . . if I were going to give this a title, I would call it simply "A Portrait of a Hero." These boys lived with death.

S.A.A.F. Pilots decorated.

One Legged Pilot wins D.S.O.

The fourth South African D.S.O. of this war has been awarded to Lieut. Douglas (Shorty) Rogan, aged 24, a fighter pilot who flies with an artificial limb.

. . . was on active service in the Middle East for only two months when he had two air craft destroyed and one damaged to his credit.

In one aerial combat he was severely wounded, but in spite of his injury he brought his aircraft safely back.

. . . he spent 2 ½ months in hospital . . .

In less than a year he was back in the Middle East with an artificial leg fitted.

He recently accounted for two probables.

Rogan is South Africa's Bader.

First to land in Sicily.

. . . three pilots (including Douglas) helped the air umbrella for the invasion of Sicily. They were among the first pilots to operate from a Landing ground on the Island four days after the bridgeheads had been established.

. . . their wing has been on of the first into battle from Cairo to Catania.

. . . their wing was the first of the Desert Air Force to go to Malta from where they escorted bombers for the softening up of Sicily.

Giving his impressions of the fighting in Sicily Lieut. Rogan said the final rounds in the battle of Catania seemed to him fiercer than the battle of Mareth.

DISTINGUISHED DIGGER

South Africa's distinguished one-legged pilot, Lieut. D.S. Rogan, D.S.O., was a promising member of the Diggers R.F.C. and played for the under 19 and third teams . . .

John Andrew Rogan:

Ian made every endeavour to be released from the Standard Bank for active service, but they would not do so, and without their permission he could not join up. He was very disappointed, and only desisted from his efforts to get enrolled for active service when it was pointed out to him that no good purpose would be served by making further efforts to enlist and that the Rogan family had suffered more than a fair share of the sorrow which had entered so many lives and homes.

Chapter 30
Pray without ceasing

1 Thess. V: 17

All Thy works shall praise Thee, O Lord, and Thy
saints shall bless Thee.
                    Psa. 145.10.
Scented air, gardens decked with flowers,
The Jacaranda mauve, 'neath blue cloudless sky,
Purple Bougainvillea, and gleaming golden showers,
        Proclaim that God is nigh.
Oh earth, a highway but not a goal,
They bounty is for man, but not to horde,
Contribution meet to the garden of the soul,
        Where dwells the Risen Lord.
Oh earth, thy music soothes, day and night,
Heart strings respond with many a cord,
Song vibrates on waves of light,
        Up to the throne of God.
Oh earth, the Truth shall ne'er decay.
The Risen Christ, by whom we are redeemed,
Shall come again on that great Day.
        By all he shall be seen.
Oh earth Thy order shall give place,
To Eternal things in a world that's new,
The redeemed shall live, a saintly race,
        In God whose word is true.

Oh earth in the world that shall be,
The saints shall rule, midst angel song,
In the love of God, and with purity
    A joyful everlasting throng.
J.R.
6.12.31   Pretoria

[The Lord is my light and my salvation; whom shall I fear? the Lord is the strength of my life; of whom shall I be afraid?
When the wicked, even mine enemies and my foes, came upon me to eat up my flesh, they stumbled and fell.
Though an host should encamp against me, my heart shall not fear: though war should rise against me, in this will I be confident.
Psalm 27:13

WAR

In vibrant tones the challenge came,
In spreading war and scorching flame,
Unflinching we met the fateful hour
The Eternal God our shield and power.
With calm resolve the nation stood,
In prayer, diffused with anxious mood,
Faith in God dispelling fear,
Like morning star the pathway clear.
'Gainst ruthless foe, intent on spoil,
Brave men fought with arduous toil
They faltered not, in bitter way,
Nor reckoned cost, or ugly scar.
The nation strove till victory's hour,
Shattering vain dreams of world power,
Give honour to our gallant men,
We'll not forget, God prosper them.
Loved ones rest in soldiers grave,
In passing, their all they gave,

Lingering thoughts dwell oft with them,
Yearning to hear their voice again.
Lord spread thy covering wings around,
Make grieving hearts they hallowed ground,
Give sorrowing lives Thy loving care
Through lonely years their burden share.
J.R.
Johannesburg
December, 1945

As thy days so shall thy strength be.
Deut. 33: 25

A faint glow in the Eastern sky
Heralds the new born day,
Twittering birds speak mate to mate
Gently the world becomes awake,
To meet the morning ray.
In prayer I yield myself to him,
Who came to earth for me,
I claim cleansing power from guilt and sin
With calm clear thought and peace within,
Throughout the busy day.
The midday hour, I know he's near
Along the crowded way.
With holy thought and calm within,
In stress of work, and city din,
He abides my stay.
Contact is kept with Christ the Lord,
Who died on Calvary's tree,
By whose great love and spirits' sword
Victory is ours in deed and word,
Throughout the busy day.
A gorgeous sky, with gold fringed clouds,
Evening's beauty in display,
All nature seeks refreshing rest,
Stars become earth's welcome guests
Jewelling the sunless way,
I speak to Christ in loving praise

Whose blood has set me free,
And thank him for His wondrous power
For joy and peace each passing hour,
Throughout the busy day.
J.R.
28.10.31

He led them forth by the right way that they might
go to a city of habitation.
Psa. 107:7

SOUTH AFRICA

I rambled o'er the land serene
With flower fringed paths on every hand,
In happy mood midst beauteous scene
In this dear sunny land.
In o'erflowing joy like happy youth
I burst forth into song,
The earth responds to love and truth,
Its beauty hides the wrong.
I laze upon the grassy banks,
My heart is full and gay,
With memories dear the Lord I thank,
For friends along the way.
Precious land, the work of God,
I love thy cloudless sky,
The mountains gran and winding road,
With air and veld so dry.
Midst gorgeous flowers on dewy ground,
I walk with footstep light,
Your mine, my own, a mutual bond,
Is ours by day and night.
Our lot is cast in southern sphere,
Sky calm and soothing blue,
Proclaiming God is ever near
And Saviour ever true.
In life beyond I'll love thee still,

Precious land of mine,
Around the throne with glory filled,
I'll praise Thee through all time.
J.R.
Johannesburg
25.4.37

'N land waar die Here jou Good voor sorg.
Deut. 11:12

SUID AFRIKA

Vir my daar is 'n land, 'n pragtige land,
Waar die voels in die bome sing,
Met breë riviere, die hele land deur
En berge wat eerbied afdwing.
Vir my daar is 'n taal, 'n soet, soet taal,
Die taal van ons pragtige land
Die mooiste toon, 'n die heue dit draal
Vir die mense en nasie 'n bond.
Vir my daar is 'n land, 'n rustige land,
Die land waar die Voortrekkers slap,
Daar 'n taal soet in toon, met sagste klank,
Vir die nasie 'n deurbare skat.
Gee my die land, die pragtige land
Die land van ons moeders so bly
Met blydskaap en vreugde die land vir ons band
Die land van die dapp re en vry.
Vir my net een land 'n pragtige land
'n land net onder die son,
Mag die Here dit seen, me oorvloedige hand,
Tot die dag die Kristus sal kom.
J.R.
Pretoria, 8.1.32

Thoughts arising out of frequent desert journeys through the:

NAMIB DESERT

At break of day the morning star
With lustre clear shines from afar,
Sunrise glow adorns the East,
A rapturous sight, a desert feast,
Fringed in gold each mountain peak
In latitudes high sentinel keep,
Unseen, the morning mists fade away,
Silence heralds another day.
Vast, solitary, drear desert land,
With covering drab of shifting sand,
Thy great expanse, no sustenance yield
Nor fruit, or flower, or harvest field,
Alone stand gnarled stunted trees,
Midst withing, blasting, scorching breeze
In cloudless sky the noonday heat
Scorches growth on sand-dunes bleak,
Rivers and spruits for water cry,
The water holes, sand-filled and dry.
In western sky midst changing scene
A ball of red sinks low, serene
Desert sand high in the air,
Lends colour to the scene so fair,
The sun forsakes its languid rays
And mountains dress in blueish haze,
Darkness steals across the land,
The parched earth with cool wind fanned,
No factory noise, or speeding trains
Disturbs the peace – silence reigns.
Midst sand-dunes high and sunshine bright,
Here life is dead as darkest night,
Yet God affords such desert land,
A place within His world plan.
The ages pass, men come and go,
God's plan evolves, silent and slow,
Gradually there comes climatic change,
Appointed times, and seasonal rains,

Rivers and spruits begin to flow,
Turbid and deep, swift and slow
On moistened earth, the grass grows green,
And cattle browse where dunes had been,
Over tilled land, the church bells ring
And happy housewives folklore sing,
The earth proclaims the Lord is here
Eternal God is always near
Contented people offerings bring
To Christ, their Lord, Redeemer, King.
J.R.
Johannesburg, 1941

Love one another as I have loved you.
St. John XV:12

Lord fill me with radiant love Divine,
In life serene may Thy beauty shine,
Use me Lord reveal Thyself through me,
Thy servant, Lord, I fain would be.
Lord of all truth, the hidden source,
Steadfast keep me, near the cross.
Come Lord in Love, and Risen power,
Light Thou my path each passing hour.
J.R.
Johannesburg, 8.5.46

Jesus said "Follow me".
St. Matt. 4:19
A stands for Allister lively and strong
L is for lovely, radiant like morn,
L also for laughter, expression of joy
I love, we love him, our fine darling boy,
S is for sunshine, he spreads all around,
Talking so wisely in sweet childish sound
E for enjoyment, at home, school, and play,
Ready and trying to be nice every day.
Thou shalt call his name John.
St. Luke 1: 13
J is for John, a precious dear boy,
Only a wee chap, he gives us great joy,
H is for happy and loving all day,
N stands for nice at home and in play.
The Lord is with Thee
St. Luke 1:28
M is for Mackenzie, a sturdy wee boy,
A lways in mischief his time to employ,
C is for chattering from morning to night
K eeping the house every cheery and bright.
I ndependent he plays, through the long day
E njoying his childhood, in his own happy way.
God is love.
1 John IV:8
A stands for Ann, a dear little babe,
N ewly arrived from heaven's sweet glade,
N ear to our hearts, with eyes soft and blue. We love
you dear Ann, because it is you.
There is a lad here.
St. John VI:9
R is for Rodney
O ur sweet baby boy
D is for darling, our delight and great joy
N stands for nestling in cosy cot warm,
E nfolded in love and protected from harm
Y is for you, our baby boy dear. A present from God,
with eyes blue and clear.

A PRAYER

Their angels do always behold the face of my Father.
St. Matt. 18:10
Dear Jesus, lovely Jesus
I've had a happy day,
In home and garden beautiful,
With lots of lovely play.
Bless my Mummie and dear Daddy
And dear wee brother/sister sweet,
And Jesus stay beside me
When in my cot I sleep.
Bless . . ..
J.R.
Johannesburg, 1948

Grandma Rogan

(Left) taken about 1940

Grandma Rogan (left), taken about 1945.

Mackie Rogan in Go-Cart.

Chapter 31
Reminiscences and Travel

Reminiscences

About 1900 a retired Caledonia Railway Engine Driver informed me that a Shunting engine on which he was working was attached for debt.

A retired C.G.R. Engine Driver informed me that the Passenger coaches on the East London – Queenstown Section during the '80s were so light and small that an unequal distribution of the load caused the vehicles to derail. His engine was a boiler on a frame without a cab.

On my first visit to the Pienaars River – Settlers Branch line the mixed train was hauled by two very small engines which were imported along with the rails during the Boer war as part of the Pretoria siege guns equipment. The train was worked by one man who combined the duties of Driver, Stoker, Conductor and Guard, in himself.

From time to time, I was employed by the "East London DAILY DESPATCH" to report verbatim political speeches. Amongst others I reported Dr. Jamieson (of Jamieson Raid fame), Dr. Smart, who was then Minister of Railways, Sir Gordon Sprigg, who was Prime Minister of the Cape at one time and a colleague of Cecil Rhodes.

At the Gaika Loop disaster (New Year's night 1910-1911) I took charge of the Breakdown arrangements, and personally disposed of the dead; 19 killed and 39 injured.

After a cloud burst followed by a tidal wave on the Buffalo River thousands of drowned snakes were washed up on the Orient Beach. It was an unforgettable sight.

During the sulphuric eruptions under the sea at Walvis Bay shoals of fish swam towards the shore with their mouths above the water level, and I saw the layers of dead fish stretching along the shore for about 20 miles. They were of all kinds and descriptions.

When I arrived at East London during 1902 Welsh steam coal was using in the Railway Engines. Indwe, Cyphergat, and Bamboo (Stormberg) coal was also used in small quantities, but owing to its calorific value two firemen had to be used on each engine.

About 1902, Mr. Aspinall, Mechanical Engineer, on the Lancashire and Yorkshire Railway, praised the boldness of the Chief Mechanical Engineer of the C.G.R. in designing such a large engine as the 8th class for work on the 3'6" gauge. He states emphatically that the Maximum Boiler, Firebox, axle load, and other limits had been reached.

There were no dining cars on the Eastern System when I arrived at East London, and I saw the first electrically lit saloons to work over the Easter System arrive at London. They were C.S.A.R. saloons.

I saw Beit Bridge being built.

About 1917, an old gent living near Waterpoort in the Zoutpansberg District, informed me:

> (a) That he was in a Commando which fought rebellious natives near Louis Trichardt. He said that the night before the battle they knelt in prayer on a kopje and promised God that if he would give them victory, they would build a church on the kopje in question. Louis Trichardt D. R. church, a landmark in the town and district now stands where these good men knelt and prayed.
> (b) He also sought President Kruger's permission to trek north of the Zoutpansberg range and permission was given by the President on the understanding that Police protection could not be afforded to him as the Transvaal Northern border was at the Soutpansberg Mountain Range. From there to the Limpopo was "no man's land".

During 1902 I saw a swarm of locusts such as the oldest residents of Sterkstroom had not previously seen in any part of Africa, and during my residence in S.W.A. I saw a swarm of voetgangers which eclipsed anything I had ever seen before. Their movements in the long grass could only be likened to the ocean swell.

I have frequently seen trains impeded by the presence of Koedoe on the line in S.W.A.

Near Karibib, S.W.A., two opposing swarms of large insects, one black and the other greenish engaged in desperate battle fighting to death. I could plainly hear their combined "piep piep"; their battle cry, or was their cry of pain.

When I landed in S. A. during 1902 the sea was at the foot of Adderly Street, Cape Town, near where the Alhambra Cinema now stands.

In the absence of a bridge the Buffalo, East London, was crossed by means of pontoon.

TRAVEL

Mum and I

During our residence in Scotland, we travelled fairly extensively in Scotland, including to most of the watering places on the Firth of Clyde, the Kyles of Bute, the Firth of Forth, not forgetting Glasgow and Edinburgh. We saw Sir Walter Scott's monument, Holy Rood Palace, Princess Street Gardens, Edinburgh, and Dumfries, where the statue of Robert Burns, the Scottish National Poet stands in the High Street, the strong flowing river Nith as it cascades towards the Solway Firth and the site of Greyfriars Church, were Robert the Bruce slew the traitor Comyn, an act of great national significance.

During out two visits from South Africa, we visited many lovely old Abbeys, ruined castles, and historical places. We were charmed with the green, well-wooded, bountifully watered countryside, intersected with burns and rivers, nevertheless we felt as though we were confined to a Doll's house and garden, and longed for the blue sky, clear pure air and the wide expanses of South Africa girded by mountain and kopje.

Between us we have seen the large rivers of Britain and Africa, we have stood beside the roaring waters of the Zambezi at the Victoria Falls, the Orange River in its great leap over the Augrabies (King George) Falls, Howick Falls, Toleni (Transkei) Falls and the other lesser water falls.

The Orange River has been crossed at Pethulie at Orange River Stations, below Kimberley, Fourteen Streams, Upington, Aliwal North, Kakaas, and Prieska. The Nyl, Limpopo, Vaal, Wit and Swart Nosop (S.P.A.) Sabie, Eland, Great Fish (One in the Cape Province and one is S.W.A.) Crocodile, Gamtoos, Kuisib (S.W.A.) Kei, Buffalo, Letaba, Keurbooms, the rivers flowing into the sea on the south coast, Natal, and several others are well known to us.

Our travels included Bulaway, Natopos, where Cecil John Rhodes lies buried, the David Livingstone Museum in Livingston, Northern Rhodesia, Port Elizabeth, where we visited the Snake Park, East London, and saw where the place, marked by a memorial plaque, on which Lieut. Bailey landed and thus opened the way for the present beautiful town.

The place where the ill-fated survivors from the wrecked troopship, S.S. Birkenhead landed and a trip by Cableway to the top of Table Mountain were seen and experienced, respectively.

A journey by bicycle (See Appendix B) from Assegai Bosch, via Tzisikama, through Knysna Forest, via Keurbooms River south, Plettenber Bay, Knysna and Wilderness (190 miles) to George, was an unforgettable experience, the scenic beauty, the combination of forest, river, mountain, and sea surpassing anything I had ever seen before.

DESERTS

I penetrated into the Kalahari Desert from the east to as far as Kuruman and the surrounding district and from the west to east of Gobabis.

Time was spent in the Karroo at Burghersdorp, and De Aar and I travelled through it by train on many occasions.

The lonesome, sand-blasted, sand-duned Namib was traversed from north south, including through a portion of the Consolidated Diamond Fields between Kolmans Kop – Pomana (where there is an X-ray installation to photograph all persons and packages leaving the fenced in area) and to Ellenboog, where a huge elbow-shaped rock jutes far out into the sea.

Mossel Bay, Lüderitz, Swakopmund and Walvis Bay Light Houses were visited, at Walvis Bay I saw the guns guarding the entrance to the Bay (1940-41) and went over a merchant ship which had a gun on the afterdeck.

Wylie's Poort and Water Poort (sand River) in the Zoutpansberg Range, Tower Water Poort, near Klipplast and other less, but well known Poorts, were traversed.

By car I travelled Cape Town to Mossel Bay, Johannesburg to East London, Pietermaritzburg through Zululand to Johannesburg via Piet Retief and Ermelo, the Transkei, Xiskei, Pondoland, Swaziland, parts of Bechuanaland and Basutoland, and practically everywhere in the Union, including through the Kruger National Park on two occasions.

By air Mum had a trip over the Zambesi Falls and I after experiencing my first flight during 1918 or 1919, from Roberts Heights over Irene, travelled by air on several occasions, Windhoek, Keetmanshoop, Kimberley – Johannesburg: [ILLEGIBLE]-Maun (Kalahari Desert), Palapye Road – Johannesburg: Johannesburg – Cape Town – Mossel Bay: and Cape Town – Port Elizabeth – East London. On one occasion when landing at Palapye Road the plane bogged, smashing the propellor giving the passengers and crew a shaking up. Arising out of the delay caused by this mishap we took off from Maun early the following morning in the pitch darkness, and the effect of the rising sun on the clouds underneath was one of the most beautiful sights I have ever seen. In the cloud shapes were seen mountain, river and valley of lovely golden hue changing gradually in colour as the sun ascended in the heavens until we looked down on a sea of fleecy white cloud.

The Copper Mines at Messina and Tsumeb (S.W.A.) were visited and I frequently passed the place (Khorab) where Beneral Botha accepted the surrender of the S.W.A. German Forces.

On one occasion I spent a day at Nelspruit in sweltering heat and the following day was spent in snow storm at Belfast.

The following is a list of the towns and dorps Mum and I visited in our travels, together and separately, excluding the places visited by my darling when in India:

England:
Bolton
Carlisle
Liverpool
London
Manchester
New Castle

Scotland:
Aberdeen
Ardrossan
Ayr
Dumfries
Dundee
Dunoon
Edinburgh
Glasgow
Greenock
Inverness
Kirkcaldy
Kirkcudbright
Largs
Moffatt
Newton Stewart
Paisley
Rothesay
Saltcoats

Ireland:
Dublin
Killarney
Queenstown

South Africa:

Alice
Aliwal North
Barberton
Belfast
Bloemfontein
Breyten
Brits
Britstown
Burghersdorp
Butterworth
Cambridge
Cape Town
Cathcart
Coligny
Craddock
Cullinan
De Aar
Duiwelskloof
Durban
Ermelo
Erasmus
Fort Beaufort
Germiston
Gordon's Bay
Graaff-Reinet

South Africa:

Grahamstown
Greytown
Harding
Humansdorp
Indwe
Johannesburg
Kalk Bay
Kimberley
King William's Town
Klerksdorp
Knysna
Kokstad
Komatipoort
Komga
Louis Trichardt
Lichtenburg
Lydenburg
Margate
Messina
Middleburg (C&T)
Molteno
Mossel Bay
Muizenberg
Naauwpoort
Nelspruit

South Africa:

Nylstroom
Oudtshoorn
Pietermaritzburg
Pietersburg
Piet Retief
Port Alfred
Port Elizabeth
Port Shepstone
Port St. John
Postmasburg
Potgietersrus
Pretoria
Prieska
Queenstown
Rosmead
Scottburg
Somerset East
Somerset Strand
Simonstown
Sterkstroom
Tzaneen
Uitenhage
Umtata
White River

Southern Rhodesia:	Northern Rhodesia:
Bulawayo	Livingstone
Bechuanaland:	South West Africa:
Kuruman	Gobabis
Mafeking	Grootfontein
Mahalapye	Kakakamas
Palapye	Keetmanshoop
Vryburg	Keimos
	Lüderitz
	Marienthal
	Okahandja
	Omaruru
	Otavi
	Otjo
	Otjiwarongo
	Rehoboth
	Swakopmund
	Walvis Bay

In our travels we stayed in over 80 different hotels in South Africa, and spent holidays in Scottburgh, Umkomaas, Warners Beach, Winkelspruit, East London, Port Elizabeth, Port Alfred, Mossel Bay, Cape town (Sea Point and Fish Hook and Gordons Bay) and Oudtshoorn.

Chapter 32
The Love and Overruling Power of God

It is recorded in the first chapter of Job that there was a day when the sons of God came to present themselves before the Lord, and Satan came also among them (uninvited, as usual) and the accuser of the Brethren accused Job, to God of being motivated by a sinful ulterior motive, in walking uprightly in the sight of God and of his fellow men. God accepted the challenge of Satan to allow Job to be tested in their fiery furnace of human distress, on the condition that Satan would not be permitted to take Job's life.

Job who had no guarantee that his next disaster would not be the last, held tenaciously to his faith in God, in whom he trusted through the terrible ordeals, and we read this his latter days were better than at the beginning. Walking with my blessed Saviour, who redeemed me on Calvary's Cross with his precious blood, I have been all too frequently aware of spiritual and physical Satanic influences, forcing me down from the glory lit heights when "in Christ" into deep valleys, where the shadows fell and temptation abounded when strength to overcome and the grace to live victoriously were weakened by Satan's persistent presence. So severe has been the struggle at time to keep steadfast on our sure foundation, even Jesus Christ, that I have sometimes wondered whether Satan has chosen me, as he did Job, for his special attentions and, whether, in order to be continually on the spot he had to set up a branch establishment in me. Be the position as it may I was conscious throughout early life, in lovely-dreamy Roucan, in Glasgow, and later, but to a lesser extent, in sunny South Africa, of a veritable furnace of temptation, where snares, pitfalls of many descriptions and hidden dangers lurked in my daily walk. But for the protecting loving care of my heavenly Father, who took care of Job, when it seemed all was for ever lost, I must, humanely speaking, have fallen and sunk to the dust perhaps never to rise again.

In those early years, although I knew it not at this time His loving Angel kept guard over me, and in Glasgow, when living in the midst of godlessness and alluring temptation to do as others did, he sent "my Angel" into my life, whose love, sweetness and ennobling influence saved me and kept me steady in my most difficult years. My heavenly Father had foreseen everything and made ample provision to prevent one of his children from taking all that he had and going into the far country.

Praise the Lord Oh my Soul for such a wonderful Saviour, who not only Redeems, but who in His Resurrection Power is able to lead us into, and in, the paths of righteousness and truth.

Satan unable to induce me to follow in his devilish worldly ways tried again and again to physically destroy me in order that he might get me out of his way, and foreseeing that I would be given the strength and grace to resist and reject his evil suggestions he commenced early in my life to pay special attention to for ever remove me out of his way as the following incidents indicate:

1. When a child I was rendered unconscious by a large stone thrown by another boy.

2. Climbing high up on the ruins of Torthorwald Castle, when about 10 years, my body was grazed by huge stones falling from the arched stone roof, high above me. I escaped instant death by a matter of 2" or 3" and at the moment was terrified by the awful and realistic awareness of the presence of an evil spirit. Children played on these ruins daily and stones were never known to fall from the roof.

3. On a dreadfully, dark, stormy night I crashed face on, in a pedestrian on the lonely Roucan Road, receiving a severe shock to my nervous system. We had a wide road at our disposal to pass each other.

4. I was struck by an open carriage door of a moving train on Maxwell Park Station platform being thrown across the platform much bruised and shaken.

5. I collided head on with another cyclist in East London, when my cycle was completely smashed.

6. Near Assegai Bosch my chauffeur-driven rail car was smashed when it collided head-on with a gangers trolley. I was thrown upwards and forwards landing heavily, very much bruised and badly shaken.

7. Near Commadagga, my rail car collided slightly with a gangers trolley.

8. The rail car in which I was travelling ran over a dog, and on another occasion a pig was the victim. On both occasions my Heavenly Father kept the car on the rails thus saving me from bodily harm, or even death. Satan had placed the animals on the rails for my destruction.

9. A passenger train in which I was travelling was involved in a head-on collision near Dasrie Deur when I was much shaken.

10. When passing over a level crossing my rail car crashed into a span of mules near Hercules. I landed heavily on my back, some distance away, amongst the kicking animals.

11. Satan's most desperate effort was the occasion on which my rail car left the rails (the cause was never established) on the steep downslope between Soekmekaar and Moeketsi when I was thrown down in the mountainside where I was found unconscious. I was very seriously injured necessitating my being away from duty for four months.

The Dr. Who gave me first aid (or didn't do so) told me that at the time he considered it was a waste of his time to attend to me, as, in his opinion I had only a few hours to live. Both the Dr. and his wife who always was a doctor, told me subsequently that I was a living miracle.

12. Leaning out of my coach on a dark night to close a door that had swung open I was horrified to see, and hear, the door crashing against the end of a bridge, leaving my outstretched arm in mid-air. Only the watchfulness and care of my Heavenly Father saved my arm from being wrenched out of its socket, in the snare set by the Evil one.

13. Near Hoedspruit, on the Selati line, the rail car ran straight into a furious grass fire on both sides of the line, on emerging from a

deep cutting. The high flames scorched my hair and eyebrows and I inhaled the flame-filled air, but fortunately the petrol did not ignite. Truly the Lord is good to such a call upon his name.

14. When pruning fruit trees in our Pretoria garden, the ladder slipped on dry leaves and in falling, I broke my wrist.

15. Near Gobabis, S.W.A., the trees amongst which I was standing were struck by a whirlwind, or was it a tornado, uprooting several of them. Only my sense of self-preservation and speed of foot saved me from serious bodily injury.

16. Near Vaalwater a large black mamba crossed my path at close quarters.

Speaking of snakes, when darling Mum was leaving India to join me in Scotland for South Africa (1910) a beautifully marked adder, whilst in the act of crossing in front of us, was killed by me. My father, who was with us and who had lived in the district practically all his life, had not previously seen one of these reptiles.

Satan entered the garden of Eden in the form of a snake to beguile Eve and thus bringing sin into the world, and I firmly believe the foregoing incidents were of Satan's origin, foreshadowing Satan's attempts to destroy our Heavenly walk with God. Again and Again he had endeavoured to destroy our domestic happiness, he has tried to poison the spiritual streams of living water and to drive us out into the wilderness of modernism, but praise the Lord, who giveth us the victory, we were imparted the strength to withstand the grace to live near to our Blessed Lord, and the joy of victory.

Bless the Lord oh my soul who has caused me to triumph over our satanic enemy and given me glorious victory through Jesus, who was tempted in all points like as we are yet without sin and who did not permit me to be tempted beyond my strength. He has never let me down, although I have all too frequently failed him and grieved the Holy Spirit.

From 24 years of age my Saviour, my Rock and my Fortress has been in control of my life, leading me upwards and onwards to higher heights and greater endeavour. He is a wonderful Saviour, more even than He claims to be and in His love and wisdom when the forces of evil were battering at the door of my soul yea, when they had got it a little bit open, He brought "My Angel" into my life and thus by her sweet, pure, loving influence, he saved me from destruction setting my feet in "The Way" of life everlasting. He led me in the Right path making me to abhor evil with a perfect abhorrence.

My environment in the Roucan and Glasgow was not altogether good without my being in any way able to alter my circumstances and I now realise that my Saviour walked beside me, striving with me, wooing me and warning me until I yielded myself wholly to Him in East London Town Hall, from which time he was Master of my life and I his willing servant.

My experience is that grace for the day's need is always available if we seek it, the Bread of Life sustains, the Water of Life is refreshing, and the Holy Spirit gives strength to go forward and continue to live in His Ever-Blessed Name.

Chapter 33
The World as I Have Experienced It

And as I see it in 1949

*C*hildhood years in sweet-dreamy-old-time Roucan, where everyone could have lived in tun with God were hard and the future prospects were not at all pleasing, Lairds, Farmers, and Gentry ground their workers down to the dust of the earth, where they kept them under the iron heel of CapitalisticLand Lord-ism supported by Britain's Tory Government. Children born on the land, lived their lives in the fields toiling for starvation wages, and died penniless, houseless, and without possessing a small piece of the land on which a house could be built, considering themselves fortunate if they escaped the necessity of having to enter the cold-soulless-pitiless workhouse from which there was no living return.

Where was the much vaunted established church of Scotland with its learned ministry – it certainly was not championing the downtrodden, honest, hard-working peasantry, who after 72 hours labour found they could not keep awake however much they strove during the full, lengthy, uninteresting discourse in church on Sundays, but it cared for, and pampered in the social circles whose lives consisted of fox hunting, holidaying, living riotously on the good of the land and in idle amusements. It was tragic and young men and maidens, the cream of the country, drifted whenever they found it possible to do so, to the towns and other centres, uncared for and unnoticed with the result that they were lost to the church, whose ministers, indifferent to the spiritual welfare of their flocks, continued to fraternise with the well-to-do and to live completely out of touch with the peasant workers.

I was a regular attendant at Sunday School, when my clothes permitted, and was compelled to attend church, which was as far as I was concerned, a meaningless-boring service in which the few worshippers did not appear to be interested. When I left the Roucan for Glasgow, the Minister did not follow me up with a letter of introduction to another church and for five impressionable years I only went to church, generally a different one each time, on a few occasions and then no one took the trouble to speak to me, or endeavour to lead me to Christ.

I have lived through three major wars, the Boer War, World War No. I and World War No. II, the former I consider was engineered by the capitalists on the Rand who were mostly Jews, and by the Imperialistic clashing aims of Britain and Germany, and to the existence of the Rand Gold Fields. Germany was manoeuvring to the get two Republics under its wing, Britain was determined to possess them and thus get control of the hidden treasure of gold, and caught between two great Empires the Republics could not escape, or avoid, war, which had to be fought in self defence and they proved themselves a brave foe, equal to the best.

In the two World wars we saw Britain, a part of the physical Israel of the Bible attacked by Satanic Aryan Forces from the German Empire against which Britain had to fight in war or perish. There was no choice – the forces of evil, under the control of Satan, having determined to exterminate the Israel people, the chosen servants of God. Wars will continue to break out at intervals as predicted by our Saviour as the enemy (Satan) is determined to thwart God's plan of World Redemption, until such time as Christ returns to assume the reins of Government as has been foretold in Scripture. Listen to the words of the Master as recorded in the 21st Chapter of St. Luke's Gospel:

> (9) When ye shall hear of wars and commotions be not terrified, for these things must first come to pass,
> . . .
> (10) . . . nation shall rise against nation, and Kingdom against Kingdom.

For many years, the British-Israel World Federation has proclaimed aloud to a headless world that World Federation, or at least Federation of the Western World, as a commencement, is the only means whereby war may be prevented and recently the same idea has been mooted in the press as thought it was an entirely new idea. But Federation or not Federation the forces of evil are determined to destroy the Israel people, who are God's serving people, and nothing can stop them in their evil purpose, but they shall not succeed and Christ's coming will put an end to Satan's power. Wars must be fought for the reason that they are forced upon Israel and also to restrain the evil foe, but each one only leaves the world in a worse state than ever before, the nation's finest manhood is slaughtered in their thousands, widows are left to grieve, and strive for a livelihood, children grow up fatherless, moral barriers are broken down, and money becomes the god of the people and nation more than ever before, with the "get rich by any means", covetous, selfish grabbers trampling on less fortunate brethren. Peace in the International spheres recedes to the far corners of the earth, the sports fields are patronised to a greater extent than ever before, Sunday has ceased to be a day of rest and worship, and men's hearts are failing them as they watch the gathering clouds in the Eastern horizon, but the Man of Peace, whose star was seen in the East, remains rejected by the Nation whom he came to redeem. The voice of the Church is a babel of modernism without appeal to the average man, who counts more than any others, and mankind drifts helplessly towards a catastrophic period such as has never before been or ever will be.

Christ said, "When ye see these things come to pass, Look up, for your salvation draweth nigh. – Look up to the Christ and not inside your rebellious heart nor your bank book, for only in Him is there redemption and His coming draweth nigh."

Staggering numbers of infantry, naval and air forces are under arms, the "atomic" race is well on the way towards perfection, e.g., a bomb that can obliterate millions in one blast, pilotless aircraft are even now skimming through the sky at over 600 miles per hour, bombers, refuelled in the air can encircle the globe without landing, new revolutions are for ever breaking out, World War No. III seems to be accepted as a certainty, the air is filled with nervous tension and doubt, and politician anxiously endeavour to delay the dread time when East and West shall meet in catastrophic conflict.

Conferences end in failure, Communism boldly challenges capitalism across the ever-narrowing border, manmade plans for peace are ever and anon being put forward, whilst the Christ of God, who alone can bring peace to a war weary world is rejected by his own.

Communism at the conclusion of war engulfed the Middle East countries, with the exception of Greece, which is precariously protected by American Troops against revolutionary forces, and sped westwards to the heart of German where Russia is firmly entrenched.

The Protestant Church is alarmed and afraid, the Roman Catholics are busy worshipping a grotesque, ugly stone image of a woman with a crown precariously perched on her head of stone, named "The Lady of Fatima" who is even now (1949) being sent from country to country. What a spectacle in the 20th century – Christ the Son of God replaced by wood and stone, and His mother the Virgin Mary. Beware, Communism, which rejects Christianity has within itself the kernel of Christ's teaching, whilst Christianity has rejected its founder, and with that faith in itself, which the Church of Christ has lost, there is every possibility of Communism sweeping Capitalism, Roman Catholic idolatry, Protestant Modernism, and the Church of England ritual into the desert oblivion.

Should that day every come (and I believe it shall come) the true followers of Christ will remain steadfast in their faith to their Redeemer and there shall arise out of the theological rubble in the midst of much persecution a new, purified church which shall indeed be the body of Christ.

In the world of today work is separated from living and from the church, personality is sold as a commercial asset, skill is marketed, people have become "things", as the natives in the early days were called by the Afrikaners' "Goeders", under economic pressure, whilst competitive commercialism and industrialism override all other considerations.

Man, who was made for God, to enjoy him for ever, has eliminated the Creator, forgetting that the earth and the fulness thereof is the Lord's. The cure is neither in circumcision nor theology, but in men becoming new creatures in Jesus Christ, glorifying God in their lives and abhorring evil.

The picture I have painted is sombre indeed, and I would not have written thus had I not believed that materialism, communism, modernism, Roman Catholic Idolatry, and war shall disappear in the glory of God when his Son, Jesus, comes in majesty, surrounded by a great company of angels and saints to reign on the earth as foretold by Himself and the two angels who assured the assembled followers in Galilee that He (the resurrected Lord) would come again in like manner. This is the hope of our perplexed, despairing humanity in the presence of ever-increasing evils. Wherefor look unto Jesus, be not dismayed and await His second Advent in calm, unwavering, watchful expectancy, for Him who will come as a thief in the night, when every eye shall see Him, and they which pierced Him. Wherefor in the midst of a crooked and perverse generation encourage one another with this blessed hope.

And they shall see the Son of Man coming in a cloud with power and great glory.
And when these things begin to come to pass (see previous verses in the chapter) then LOOK UP and lift up your heads, for your Redemption draweth night.
St. Luke 21: 728

Sing, O heavens; and be joyful, O earth; and break forth into singing, O mountains; for the Lord hath comforted his people, and will have mercy upon his afflicted.
Hast thou not known? Hast thou not heard that the everlasting God, the Lord, the Creator of the ends of the earth, fainteth not, neither is weary? There is no searching of his understanding.
He giveth power to the faint; and to them that have no might he giveth strength.
Even the youths shall faint and be weary, and the young men shall utterly fall:
But they that wait upon the Lord shall renew their strength; they shall mount up with wings as eagles; they shall run and not be weary; and they shall walk, and not faint.
Trust ye in the Lord for ever; for in the Lord JEHOVAH is everlasting strength.
Isaiah 49:13; 40:2831; 26:4

Chapter 34
Fine Things I Have Read

Give Us Men

Give us men!

Men from every rank,

Fresh and free and frank;

Men of thought and reading,

Men of light and leading,

Men of loyal breeding,

The nation's welfare speeding;

Men of faith and not of fiction,

Men of lofty aim in action;

Give us men — I say again,

Give us men!

Give us men!

Strong and stalwart ones;

Men whom highest hope inspires,

Men whom purest honor fires,

Men who trample self beneath them,

Men who make their country wreath them

As her noble sons,

Worthy of their sires;

Men who leave behind them

Footprints on the sands of time,

Footprints which perhaps another,

Sailing o'er life's solemn main,

Some forlorn and shipwrecked brother,

Seeing, may take heart again;

Men who, when the tempest gathers,

Grasp the standard of their fathers

In the thickest fight;

Men who strike for home and altar,

(Let the coward cringe and falter,)

God defend the right!

True as truth though lorn and lonely,

Tender, as the brave are only,

Men who tread where saints have trod,

Men for Country, Home -- and God:

Give us men — I say again — again,

Give us men!

Bishop of Exeter

[Actually, Josiah Gilbert Holland]

The Bairnies Cuddle Doon

The bairnies cuddle doon at nicht
Wi' muckle faucht an' din.
"O, try an' sleep, ye waukrife rogues;
Your faither's comin' in."
They never heed a word I speak;
I try to gie a froon,
But aye I hap them up an' cry,
"O, bairnies, cuddle doon."
Wee Jamie wi' the curly heid—
He aye sleeps next the wa'—
Bangs up an' cries, "I want a piece"—
The rascal starts them a'.
I rin an' fetch them pieces, drinks,
They stop awee the soun',
Then draw the blankets up an' cry,
"Noo, weanies, cuddle doon."
But, ere five minutes gang, wee Rab
Cries oot frae 'neath the claes:
"Mither, mak' Tam gie ower at ance,
He's kittlin' wi' his taes."
The mischief's in that Tam for tricks,
He'd bother half the toon;
But, still, we hap them up an' cry,
"O, bairnies, cuddle doon."
At length they hear their faither's fit;
An', as he steeks the door,
They turn their faces to the wa'
While Tam pretends to snore.
"Hae a' the weans been gude?" he asks,
As he pits aff his shoon.
"The bairnies, John, are in their beds,
An' lang since cuddled doon."
An' just afore we bed oorsels,
We look at oor wee lambs;
Tam has his airm roun' wee Rab's neck,
An' Rab his airm roun' Tam's.

I lift wee Jamie up the bed,
An', as I straik each croon,
I whisper, till my heart fills up,
"O, bairnies, cuddle doon."
The bairnies cuddle doon at nicht,
Wi' mirth that's dear to me.
But soon the big warl's cark an' care,
Will quaten doon their glee.
Yet, come what will to ilka ane,
May He who rules aboon,
Aye whisper, through their pows be bald,
Oh bairnies, cuddle doon.
Alexander Anderson

GENERAL SMUTS in bidding farewell to the First Contingent of the South African Volunteers who sailed for Abyssinia July, 1940:

In taking part in this war, we are not merely defending ourselves, our country, our future, we are also standing by our friends, in the Commonwealth of nations, in all loyalty and good faith, as we know they will stand by us.

But we are doing more; we are also safeguarding that larger tradition of human freedom, of freedom of conscience, freedom of thought and freedom of religion which is today threatened as never before in history by the Nazi menace. That tradition is the spiritual rock whence we are hewn.

We have fought for our freedom in the past, we now go forth as Crusaders, as child of the cross to fight for freedom itself, the freedom of the human spirit, the free choice of the human individual to shape his own life according to the light that God has given him.

The world cause of freedom is also our cause, and we shall wage this war for human freedom until God's victory crowns the end.

I have nothing to offer but blood, toil, tears and sweat . . . You ask me what is our policy? I will say: It is to wage war, by sea, land, and air with all our might, and with all the strength that God can give us.

You ask me what is our aim? I can answer one word, Victory, Victory at all costs, VICTORY, in spite of terror, Victory, however long and hard the road may be for without victory there is no survival for the British Empire, no survival for what the British empire stood for, no survival for the urge and impulse of the ages, that mankind will move forwards towards its goal.

Winston Churchill

r

WORK

There is no satisfaction comparable to that of accomplishment.

There can be no accomplishment without work.

Ask any important man what he has enjoyed most in his life. He will tell you it was his work.

Listen to the conversation of men. It is chiefly about their work – either work accomplished, or work that they plan to do.

If your work does not interest you, either something is the matter with the work, or something is the matter with you.

There must be drudgery in all tasks. But if you bear in mind that the days of drudgery are merely days of preparation for achievement, they will not seem nearly so tedious.

Disinclination to work makes more failures than liquor or gambling. It keeps more men down than ill-health, or poverty.

The vice of the human race is laziness, and no man is so unhappy as he who is constitutionally opposed to any form of toil.

No recreation is worthwhile unless it involves work. The man who plays chess toils ten times as hard over a game as the average man does over his daily task.

Neither football, nor golf, nor tennis can be played successfully without long and hard work in preparation.

You have got to work in this world whether you like it or not. So you might as well learn to like it. You will get far more enjoyment out of it, and stand a far better chance of succeeding in it if you do.

(Copied)

FINIS

Appendix A
Genealogy

James Rogan, my grandfather, was of Irish descent, and Mary King, whom he married in Scotland came from a pure Scotch family, who had resided in Roucan Village for many generations.

James King, my great grandfather was wounded in the Battle of Waterloo in 1815.

Father, the eldest son of the marriage, married Margaret Stewart of Johnstone Village, near Lockerbie, Dumfriesshire, in 1872---a loveable, patient, sweet woman, whose generosity within her meagre means was taken advantage of to the full by the many tramps who wandered aimlessly along the country roads.

My Darling's father, Andrew G. Smith, came from a highly respected Scotch family, in the parish of Whamphray, Dumfriesshire, and her mother, Margaret Mackenzie, a very beautiful, cultured woman hailed from Inverness, where her Gaelic parents were highly respects, and much esteemed, citizens.

Our parents, honest, hard-working and thrifty lived in a hard Century, when Toryism, the forerunner of Capitalism was rampant, and men, who toiled from daylight to dark were unable to earn sufficient money to adequately provide for their families, the wealth of the land being held in the grasp of the Landowners.

Genealogical Tree

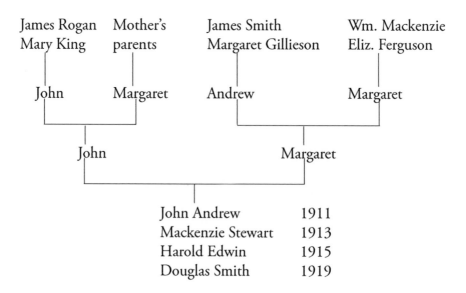

James Rogan   Mother's   James Smith   Wm. Mackenzie
Mary King   parents   Margaret Gillieson   Eliz. Ferguson

John   Margaret   Andrew   Margaret

John   Margaret

John Andrew	1911
Mackenzie Stewart	1913
Harold Edwin	1915
Douglas Smith	1919

**Roll of Honour:
Killed**

Mackenzie Stewart	1943
Harold Edwin	1944

Mum and Dad Rogan

~1945

Mum and Dad Rogan, ~1943

Appendix B

During August 1916 Mr. E. Renton, also a railwayman, and myself cycled from Assegia Bosch, in the Humansdorp District via Sheppard's Rush, Tsizikama, Bleaukrantz, Cove, Keurbooms River, Pletternberg Bay, Knysna, and wilderness to George, the distance being approximately 190 miles, and the following extracts are from letters written by Mr. Renton to his two children:

"John and I started on our journey from Assegai Bosch on Friday the 4th instant, and climbed the steep ascent from the railway, through the village to a neck between the two mountain peaks. . . . we overtook an ox wagon and enjoyed a welcome life over the last heavy mile to the summit.

. . . one tyre was flat on the whole journey we mended 17 punctures, and at Knysna the machines had to go into shops for repairs.

The road from the neck was rutty so that our progress on the down gradient was retarded, and we reached Witte Els-Bosch, 16 miles from Assegai Bosch, in the dark, where we put up with a family for the night. A Mahogany tree had just been felled, but the timber hereabouts consists mainly of Yellowwood, Ironwood, Stinkwood, Sneezewood, and Assegaiwood.

The food was rough.

Storms River – 18 miles – was reached after eight hours hard pedalling over an atrocious road, through the lovely Storms River pass, amidst scenery of indescribable grandeur. The stream itself is of delightfully clear water, making a mad rush for the sea through forest glades, over cataracts and amongst ferns.

A break in the forest gives space for the residence of the Forest Officer, a police station and two residences, with a sawmill in the distance. This is Tsizikama.

Leaving Tsizikama we could see the towering peaks of the Outeniqua range.

By this time, we looked like tramps, but the grandeur of the scenery through Blaaukrantz and Kuthing Rivers compensated for everything else. The scenery was superb, with birds of brilliant plumage. There were King Fishers and Lorries and whip-poor-wills, woodpeckers, and woodcutters.

At Coldstream, there is a large sawmill, and passing through we entered a beautiful pass with a deep flowing river running through gorges. We scarcely ever met a person or vehicle.

We now entered the Keurbooms River Pass and in the distance Plettenberg Bay came into view.

Crossing Keurbooms River on a pontoon we put up for the night at the Pontoon Boarding House and in the morning cycled via Gans Valley, and Formosa to Plettenberg Bay, where we were shewn round the whaling station (since closed down) and saw nine whales which had been landed the previous day.

Knysna was reached the same afternoon, and the Hotel Proprietor refused us admittances to the hotel on account of travel-stained appearance. We travelled on the mountain railway and saw through the Railway Sleeper Factor. We were then taken round the Bay in a motor launch, landing at the Heads where we had tea and cake. Knysna Harbour is lovely, and The Heads are glorious.

Leaving Knysna on the 9th of August, we crossed the river in a pontoon and commenced the long tedious climb up the Phantom Pass. After traversing four mountain passes, we reached "The Wilderness" and round to the Ebb and Flow of Touws River. The Wilderness is extremely lovely, and the nearby mouth of the Kaaiman's River is just too beautiful for words. We wound up this river to tis confluence with the Zwartz River and found ourselves in a deep circular basis with frowning precipices 300' high. Here we saw many forms of bird life.

We reached George, 12 miles from Wilderness, after much climbing and winding, but we were now physically fit for anything.

We visited the old Cathedral and many places of interest in this beautiful old town, joined the train for Mossel Bay, where we spent the week-end and reached Port Elizabeth, by train, after nine days memorable travelling by cycle, from Assegai Bosch to George, through the most perfect scenery in South Africa, over atrocious mud tracks, up steep winding passes, over deep, fast flowing rivers and through cool forest glade.

Appendix C

Ian Mackenzie Rogan ("Mack") – Mar 3, 1943 – April 27, 2019 ("Freedom Day")

Obituary written by Charles Breckon

We are deeply saddened to announce the passing of our esteemed colleague and dear friend, Mack Rogan. An exceptional figure in orthopedic surgery, Mack leaves behind a legacy of innovation, education, and selfless service.

Mack's tireless dedication to his work was extraordinary. Starting with the AMK total knee replacement, he moved on to champion the Low Contact Stress (LCS) total knee replacement, which became his standard procedure. Between 1989 and 2011, he performed no less than 1,800 total knee replacements, marking him as a pioneer in his field. He also performed over 400 unicompartmental knee replacements, constantly pushing the boundaries of knee surgery once he had fully understood the technique and studied the published data.

He generously shared his knowledge, serving as an international consultant to DePuy International and participating in the advanced LCS Learning Centre. Mack also took on the role of a mentor, training many junior consultants, and taking on a "fellow" every year to teach them the art and science of knee surgery.

Mack never shied away from new techniques and approaches. When computer-assisted surgery emerged, he took it in stride, teaching other knee surgeons this new procedure. He was also among the first surgeons to embrace "patient-specific" cutting jigs for total knee replacement. In his pursuit of excellence, he consistently reviewed his work, seeking improvements to provide the best possible outcomes for his patients.

Mack's exceptional leadership skills came to the fore when he served as chairperson on the hospital committee at Morningside MediClinic in 2009. He retired in 2011 but continued to serve in a semi-retired position until the age of 72. Even after leaving Morningside MediClinic, his commitment to the community led him to work part-time at Tintswalo Hospital as part of an outreach program.

But Mack was more than just a dedicated surgeon; he was a man of deep kindness. He sponsored the education of an employee's son and found work for his golf caddy at a construction company. Beyond his professional life, Mack had a deep love for trout fishing, birding, and indigenous trees. I recall a trip with him for an LCS computer-assisted surgery trip in Newcastle, where we spent extra days birdwatching in Wakkerstroom. Mack's passion for these creatures was palpable when we found Botha's Lark on the second day.

Mack's love for the outdoors extended to Finsbury Estate, his quiet retreat in Lydenburg/Mashishing, where he spent many weekends. When he found out that our colleague Prof Hans Myburgh had been confined to a wheelchair due to an accident, Mack took it upon himself to arrange regular trout fishing outings for him at Finsbury.

Mack was indeed the eternal Braveheart, always ready for the next journey. Just a day before his passing, he said to me, "Well Charlie, I'm ready for the next part of my journey in life." His courage and readiness to embrace the unknown were truly remarkable.

In his passing, we lose a great surgeon, mentor, friend, and a brave heart. Mack, we will miss you. As you embark on your next journey, travel well, dear friend.